SUPER EASY DASH DIET COOKBOOK FOR SENIORS

A 4-Week Plan with Simple, Budget Friendly Recipes to Support Heart Health, Boost Energy, and Feel Younger Everyday

Helen Parker

Disclaimer

This cookbook is intended for informational and educational purposes only. It is not a substitute for professional medical advice, diagnosis, or treatment. Seniors are encouraged to consult with a licensed healthcare professional before making changes to their diet, medications, or lifestyle routines.

The recipes and guidance in this book reflect nutritional research and best practices available at the time of publication. Because scientific understanding of diet, blood pressure, and senior wellness continues to evolve, neither the author nor the publisher can be held responsible for any adverse effects that may result from the use or application of the information provided.

Individuals managing chronic conditions such as high blood pressure, diabetes, kidney disease, or heart concerns, as well as those taking prescription medications, should seek personalized advice from their healthcare provider to ensure these recipes and dietary suggestions are suitable for their unique needs.

Table of Contents

Welcome to Your DASH Kitchen _____ 1

DASH in Simple Terms: How It Helps Seniors Thrive _____ 1

The Easy DASH Plate: Visual Guide + Grocery Staples _____ 4

Energizing Breakfast _____ 7

Herb Egg Bake Squares _____ 7

Vanilla Chia Cups _____ 8

Bell Pepper Egg Skillet _____ 9

Berry–Nut Yogurt Crunch Bowl _____ 10

Zucchini Potato Hash _____ 11

Corn Meal Mini Pancakes _____ 12

Avocado & Smoked Salmon Toast _____ 13

Cottage Cheese & Pear Bowl _____ 14

Cinnamon Rice & Breakfast Bowl _____ 15

Golden Turmeric With Latte Milk _____ 16

Cheddar Broccoli Egg Cups _____ 17

Cottage Cheese & Pineapple Cups _____ 18

Almond Dates Energy Bites _____ 19

Pear Ginger Smoothie _____ 20

Comforting Soups & Fresh Salads _____ 21

Creamy Tomato Basil Soup _____ 21

Carrot Lentil Soup With Oil Drizzle _____ 22

Broccoli Soup With Cauli Flower _____ 23

Summer Strawberry & Spinach Salad _____ 24

Roasted Beet & Walnut Salad _____ 25

Greek Chickpea Salad With Cucumber _____ 26

Quinoa Kale Bowl With Vinaigrette _____ 27

Warm Barley & Mushroom Salad _____ 28

Brown Rice & Pepper Bowl_____ 29

Watermelon Cucumber Salad _____ 30

Tuna & White Bean Salad _____ 31

Cabbage Carrot Slaw & Yoghurt Dressing _____ 32

Sweet Corn & Potato Cheddar _____ 33

Roasted Zucchini & Tomato Salad _____ 34

Apple Walnut Kale Slaw_____ 35

Wholesome Mains_____ 37

Lemon Baked COD With Spinach_____ 37

Chicken with Rosemary _____ 38

Turkey Tomato Skillet _____ 39

Herb Crusted TilapiaWith Dijon Mustard _____ 40

Chicken BakeWith Olives _____ 41

Grilled Mackerel With Swiss Chard _____ 42

Simple Lentil Sweet Potato Bowl _____ 43

Pumpkin Red Lentil Stew_____ 44

Shrimp Stir-Fry with Snap Peas & Carrots_____ 45

Cauliflower Mash With Pasta _____ 46

Mushroom Asparagus Rice Skillet _____ 47

Roasted Bell Peppers With Brown Rice _____ 48

Turkey Meatballs With Tomato-Basil _____ 49

Grilled Eggplant With Mozzarella _____ 50

Garlic Herb Trout With Lemon _____ 51

Gentle Drinks & Infusions _____ 53

Watermelon–Mint Infusion _____ 53

Warm Lemon–Honey Water_____ 53

Almond Milk Golden Latte _____ 54

Hibiscus–Berry Iced Tea _____ 54

Cucumber–Lime Sparkling Water _____ 55

Apple–Cinnamon Herbal Infusion _____ 55

Ginger–Lemon Morning Tonic _____ 56

Strawberry–Basil Infused Water _____ 56

Blueberry–Lavender Calm Tea _____ 57

Iced Green Tea with Citrus & Mint _____ 57

Peach–Rosemary Spritzer _____ 58

Spiced Apple–Ginger Warmer _____ 58

Coconut–Pineapple Refresher _____ 59

Chamomile–Vanilla Evening Tea _____ 59

Snacks and Small Bites _____ 61

Red Pepper & Walnut Spread _____ 61

Garlic Bean Spread and Crackers _____ 61

Cottage Cheese & Peach Bowl _____ 62

Roasted Edamame with Smoked Paprika _____ 62

Crispy Chickpea Bites with Herbs _____ 63

Baked Sweet Potato Fries _____ 63

Roasted Carrot Sticks _____ 64

Baked Zucchini Chips _____ 64

Hummus–Cucumber Roll-Ups _____ 65

Mini Pita Pizzas with Spinach & Tomato _____ 65

Peach & Almond Energy Bites _____ 66

Stuffed Cherry Tomatoes _____ 66

Delightful & DASH Desserts _____ 67

Citrus Yogurt Parfait _____ 67

Berry–Nut Oat Bars _____ 67

Choco Almond Clusters _____ 68

Blueberry–Lemon Yogurt Whip _____ 68

Spiced Pear Compote with Walnuts _____ 69

Baked Apple with Cinnamon & Oats _____ 69

Raspberry–Pudding _____ 70

Honey Bark with Nuts _____ 70

Baked Apricot Halves _____ 71

Cocoa–Banana Mousse _____ 71

Honey Yoghurt Cups _____ 72

Strawberry Almond Cups_____ 72

DASH Tools for Everyday Success _____ 73

Your Gentle 4-Week Meal Path_____ 73

Sodium & Blood Pressure Tracker _____ 76

Senior Swaps: Gentle Adjustments for Everyday Cooking_____ 77

Pantry Essentials at a Glance_____ 78

CONCLUSION_____ 79

Welcome to Your DASH Kitchen

Imagine walking into your kitchen and knowing that in just 20 minutes you'll have a meal that is **good for your heart, easy on your body, and satisfying to eat**. That's the promise of this book.

Cooking at home often feels overwhelming: too many steps, too much cleanup, or too many ingredients to remember. This cookbook removes those barriers. Every recipe here is:

- **Quick:** Active prep and cooking time is about 20 minutes.
- **Simple:** Only 5–7 main ingredients, plus everyday basics like olive oil or pepper.
- **Clear:** Numbered instructions, never long paragraphs.
- **Senior-friendly:** Gentle swaps for easier chewing, lighter seasoning, and lower effort.

Eating well at any age should not feel like a burden. Instead, it should feel like an act of self-care and enjoyment. Cooking the DASH way is less about dieting and more about nourishing yourself with foods that keep you strong and steady.

DASH in Simple Terms: How It Helps Seniors Thrive

The DASH Diet stands for **Dietary Approaches to Stop Hypertension**. It was developed by doctors and researchers who studied which foods naturally help lower blood pressure. But DASH is more than just numbers. It's about creating meals that make you feel **energized, comfortable, and nourished** every day.

Here's why the DASH Diet works so well, especially for seniors:

1. Balances Blood Pressure

High blood pressure is common with age, and it can silently strain the heart, blood vessels, and kidneys. DASH helps by lowering sodium (salt) and adding potassium-rich foods that relax blood vessel walls and ease circulation. This lowers the risk of strokes and heart problems while keeping energy steady.

Helpful foods:

- Bananas and oranges (potassium-rich fruits)
- Spinach and Swiss chard (leafy greens)
- White beans and lentils (plant proteins)
- Sweet potatoes (naturally high in potassium)

2. Strengthens the Heart and Brain

Healthy fats in the DASH Diet protect circulation and keep cholesterol in balance. They also improve memory, focus, and mood. Omega-3 fatty acids, in particular, are vital for brain health and reducing the risk of heart disease.

Helpful foods:

- Salmon, trout, and sardines (omega-3 fatty fish)
- Walnuts and almonds (heart-healthy nuts)
- Olive oil (replaces butter or lard)
- Flaxseeds and chia seeds (plant-based omega-3s)

3. Protects Bones and Teeth

The DASH Diet supplies calcium, magnesium, and vitamin D from both dairy and non-dairy sources. These nutrients strengthen bones, reduce fractures, and keep teeth healthy, which is especially important as bone density naturally decreases with age.

Helpful foods:

- Low-fat milk, yogurt, or fortified soy milk
- Leafy greens like kale and collard greens
- Canned salmon with bones (rich in calcium)
- Tofu made with calcium sulfate

4. Keeps Digestion Comfortable

Digestion often slows down with age, leading to constipation and discomfort. Fiber-rich DASH foods keep things moving, support healthy gut bacteria, and also help control blood sugar — a bonus for seniors managing diabetes.

Helpful foods:

- Oats and barley (fiber-rich whole grains)
- Apples, pears, and prunes (gentle fruits for digestion)
- Lentils, black beans, and chickpeas (plant proteins with fiber)
- Carrots and broccoli (high-fiber vegetables)

5. Maintains Energy and Independence

DASH meals provide slow, steady energy instead of sugar highs and crashes. This makes it easier to stay active, take walks, do errands, and enjoy daily life. Cooking simple DASH meals also helps seniors remain independent instead of relying on salty, packaged foods.

Helpful foods:

- Brown rice, quinoa, and whole wheat bread (steady carbs)
- Berries and apples (quick snacks with natural sugar + fiber)
- Eggs (easy, quick protein for any meal)
- Chicken or turkey breast (lean proteins for sustained energy)

6. Supports Healthy Weight

DASH naturally promotes balanced portions with foods that fill you up without excess calories. Maintaining a healthy weight reduces joint pain, supports mobility, and lowers risks of diabetes and heart disease.

Helpful foods:

- Leafy greens and cucumbers (filling, low-calorie veggies)
- Berries and melon (sweet treats with fewer calories than baked goods)
- Beans and lentils (fiber + protein to keep you full)
- Air-popped popcorn (a crunchy, guilt-free snack)

The Easy DASH Plate: Visual Guide + Grocery Staples

Instead of memorizing long rules, picture your plate divided like this:

- **½ plate vegetables and fruit:** Bright colors, soft textures, and natural sweetness. (Spinach, broccoli, carrots, apples, peaches.)
- **¼ plate lean protein:** Fish, chicken, beans, lentils, or tofu. Choose options that cook quickly.
- **¼ plate whole grains:** Brown rice, oats, quinoa, or whole wheat pasta, steady energy that keeps you full.
- **A drizzle or sprinkle of extras:** Olive oil, nuts, seeds, low-fat dairy, or yogurt add richness and variety.

Senior-Friendly Pantry Staples

Category	Examples (Easy & Accessible)	Tips & Uses
Freezer Allies	Frozen spinach, peas, mixed berries, chopped onions	Add spinach to soups, peas to stir-fries, berries to yogurt, onions to sauces
Canned Convenience	Low-sodium beans, lentils, tuna, diced tomatoes	Toss beans into salads, mash lentils for spreads, mix tuna with herbs, use tomatoes in quick stews
Grain Basics	Rolled oats, whole wheat pita, brown rice, barley, couscous	Use oats for breakfast bakes, pita for wraps, rice or couscous for easy sides
Flavor Builders	Olive oil, vinegar, garlic powder, lemon juice, dried herbs	Drizzle oil over veggies, splash vinegar in soups, season with herbs instead of salt
Quick Proteins	Greek yogurt, cottage cheese, eggs, chicken breasts, salmon fillets	Enjoy yogurt as a snack, eggs for fast meals, chicken or salmon for one-pan dinners
Nut & Seed Boosters	Almonds, walnuts, chia seeds, flaxseeds	Sprinkle on salads, stir into oatmeal, or blend into smoothies

Energizing Breakfast

Herb Egg Bake Squares

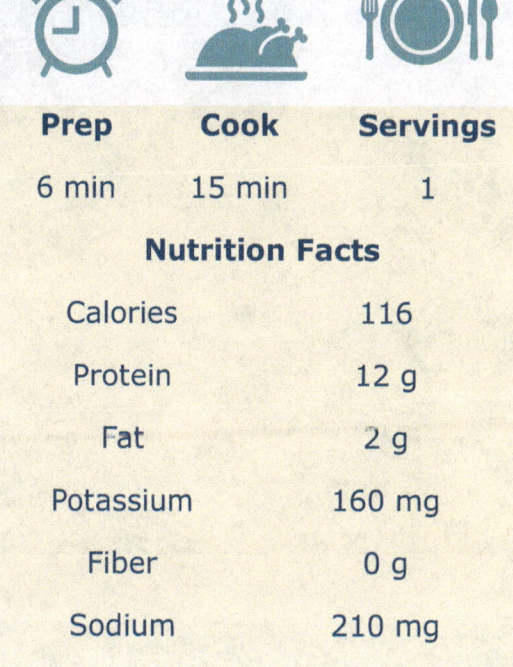

Prep	Cook	Servings
6 min	15 min	1

Nutrition Facts

Calories	116
Protein	12 g
Fat	2 g
Potassium	160 mg
Fiber	0 g
Sodium	210 mg

Ingredients

- 5 large eggs
- ¼ cup low-fat milk
- ¼ cup reduced-fat mozzarella, shredded
- 2 tbsp fresh parsley, chopped
- ¼ tsp black pepper

Senior Wellness Boost: A protein-rich breakfast that helps maintain lean muscle and supports steady morning energy.

Instructions

1. Preheat oven to 375°F (190°C) and lightly grease a small baking dish.
2. Whisk eggs, milk, and pepper in a bowl until smooth.
3. Stir in mozzarella cheese and chopped parsley.
4. Pour mixture into the prepared dish.
5. Bake for 15 minutes, or until set and lightly golden.
6. Cool slightly, cut into squares, and serve warm.

Flavor Tip: Add a sprinkle of chopped chives or parsley after baking.

Vanilla Chia Cups

Prep	Chill	Servings
10 min	2 hours	½ cup

Nutrition Facts	
Calories	180
Protein	6 g
Fat	1 g
Potassium	180 mg
Fiber	7 g
Sodium	70 mg

Ingredients

- 3 tbsp chia seeds
- 1 cup low-fat milk
- ½ tsp vanilla extract
- 1 tsp honey or maple syrup for gentle sweetness
- ¼ cup blueberries, rinsed and lightly crushed for topping

Senior Wellness Boost: Chia seeds bring omega-3s and fiber that help lower cholesterol, and support heart rhythm.

Instructions

1. In a jar or bowl, combine chia seeds, milk, vanilla, and honey. Stir well to coat seeds evenly and prevent clumping, ensuring smooth soaking.

2. Cover and refrigerate for at least 2 hours until thick and creamy.

3. Stir before serving to ensure a smooth, creamy texture and even flavor throughout.

4. Spoon into bowls or cups and top with fresh blueberries and a drizzle of honey.

Flavor Tip: Stir in a few drops of pure almond or coconut extract.

Bell Pepper Egg Skillet

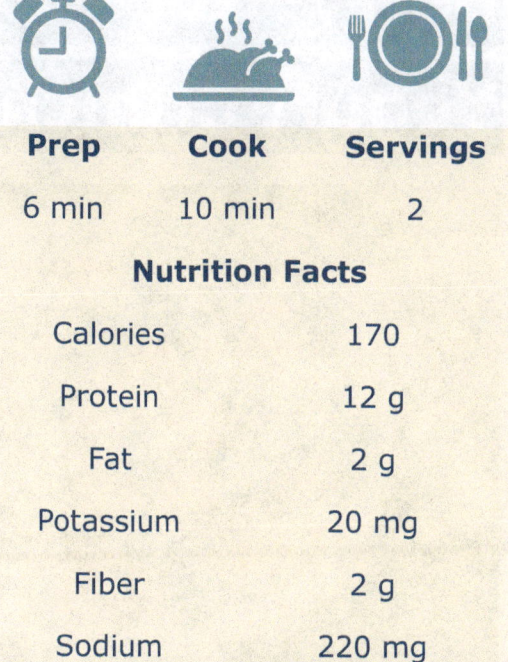

Prep	Cook	Servings
6 min	10 min	2

Nutrition Facts

Calories	170
Protein	12 g
Fat	2 g
Potassium	20 mg
Fiber	2 g
Sodium	220 mg

Ingredients

- 3 eggs
- ½ cup red and green bell peppers, finely diced for color and crunch
- ¼ cup onion, finely diced to enhance flavor
- 1 tsp olive oil, for sautéing the vegetables evenly
- ¼ tsp black pepper

Senior Wellness Boost: Loaded with vitamin C and antioxidants from peppers to boost immunity, protect vision, and promote healthy circulation.

Instructions

1. Heat olive oil in a medium skillet over medium heat. Add chopped onion and bell pepper, cooking for 3–4 minutes until softened and fragrant.

2. Crack the eggs directly into the skillet and gently scramble with a spatula, mixing the vegetables evenly.

3. Season lightly with black pepper for flavor.

4. Stir until the eggs are fully set and fluffy, about 5 minutes. Serve warm.

Flavor Tip: Top with a spoonful of salsa or sliced avocado.

Berry–Nut Yogurt Crunch Bowl

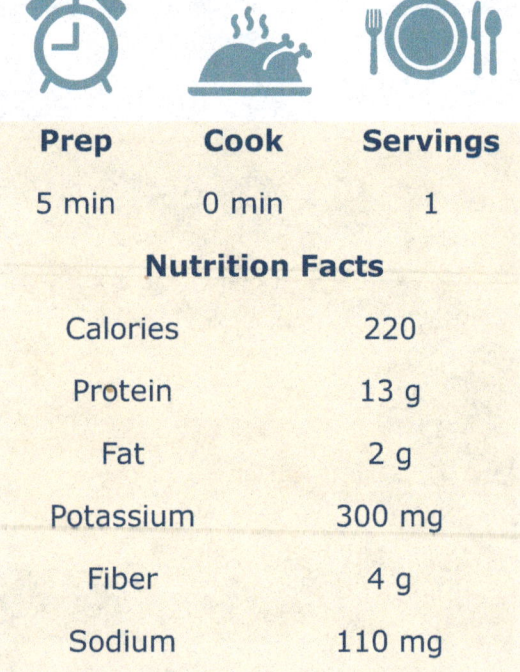

Prep	Cook	Servings
5 min	0 min	1

Nutrition Facts

Calories	220
Protein	13 g
Fat	2 g
Potassium	300 mg
Fiber	4 g
Sodium	110 mg

Ingredients

- ¾ cup low-fat Greek yogurt
- ½ cup mixed berries
- 2 tbsp unsalted nuts (almonds, walnuts, or pecans), chopped
- 1 tbsp rolled oats
- ½ tsp honey or maple syrup

Senior Wellness Boost: This recipe nourishes gut health, balances blood pressure, and provides steady energy.

Instructions

1. Spoon the yogurt into a small serving bowl, spreading it evenly so it forms a smooth base.

2. Add the berries on top, then sprinkle with nuts and oats for crunch and texture.

3. If you like a touch of sweetness, drizzle lightly with honey.

4. Chill for a few minutes before serving.

Flavor Tip: Drizzle with honey or maple syrup for natural sweetness.

Zucchini
Potato Hash

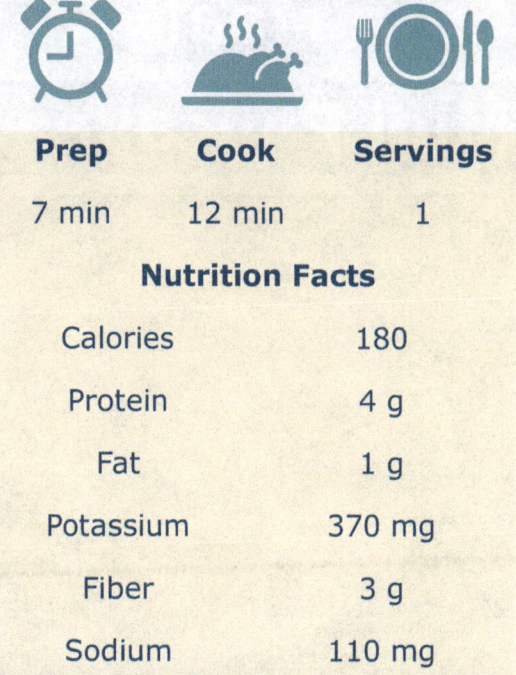

Prep	Cook	Servings
7 min	12 min	1

Nutrition Facts

Calories	180
Protein	4 g
Fat	1 g
Potassium	370 mg
Fiber	3 g
Sodium	110 mg

Ingredients

- 1 cup zucchini, diced into small, even cubes for quick cooking
- 1 cup potato, diced finely for a tender, golden texture
- ¼ cup onion, diced finely for mild sweetness
- 1 tsp olive oil
- ¼ tsp paprika for gentle and warmth of colors

Senior Wellness Boost: Packed with potassium and fiber to reduce blood pressure, aid digestion, and keep you feeling full longer.

Instructions

1. Heat olive oil in a medium skillet over medium heat. Add diced potato and cook about 6 minutes, stirring occasionally, until softened and golden.

2. Add zucchini and onion, cooking another 5–6 minutes until tender and lightly browned.

3. Sprinkle with paprika and toss well to coat.

4. Serve hot from the skillet for a hearty, flavorful breakfast to enjoy your mornings.

Flavor Tip: Add a pinch of smoked paprika or chili flakes on top.

Corn Meal
Mini Pancakes

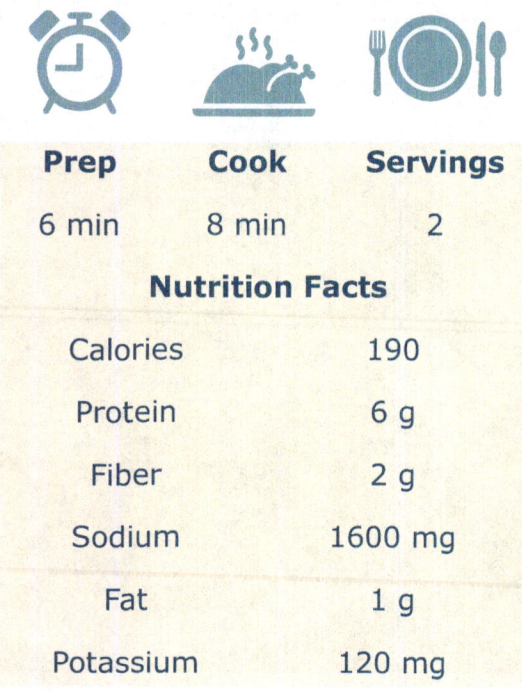

Prep	Cook	Servings
6 min	8 min	2

Nutrition Facts	
Calories	190
Protein	6 g
Fiber	2 g
Sodium	1600 mg
Fat	1 g
Potassium	120 mg

Ingredients

- 🍳 ½ cup cornmeal, finely ground for a light, tender texture
- 🍳 1 egg
- 🍳 ¼ cup low-fat milk, at room temperature for smooth mixing
- 🍳 1 tsp olive oil
- 🍳 ¼ tsp cinnamon, for a warm, subtle sweetness

Senior Wellness Boost: Whole-grain cornmeal offers lasting energy and helps stabilize blood sugar levels for a balanced morning start.

Instructions

1. In a medium bowl, whisk cornmeal, egg, milk, and cinnamon until the batter is completely smooth.

2. Warm olive oil in a nonstick skillet over medium heat, coating the surface evenly.

3. Spoon small rounds of batter into the pan, leaving space so they don't touch.

4. Cook for 2 to 3 minutes per side, until edges set and both sides turn golden. Serve warm and drizzle honey if you like.

Flavor Tip: Stir in fresh blueberries or diced apples for a juicy pop of sweetness and a touch of color in every pancake.

Avocado & Smoked Salmon Toast

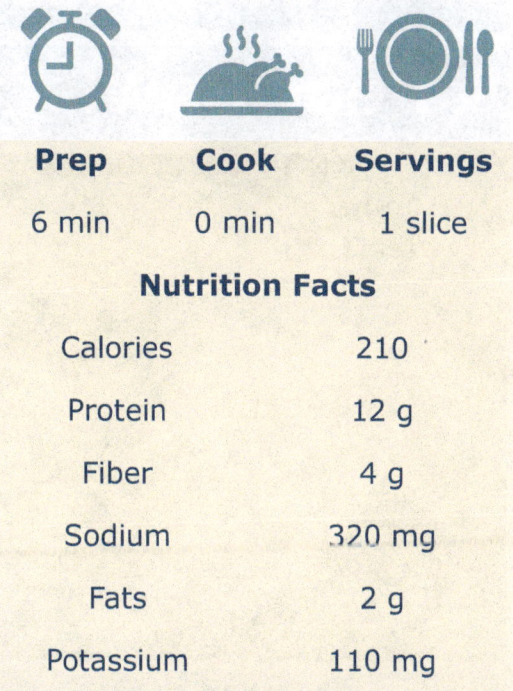

Prep	Cook	Servings
6 min	0 min	1 slice

Nutrition Facts

Calories	210
Protein	12 g
Fiber	4 g
Sodium	320 mg
Fats	2 g
Potassium	110 mg

Ingredients

- 1 slice whole-grain bread, toasted until golden
- ¼ avocado, mashed smoothly for a creamy base
- 1 oz smoked salmon, thinly sliced
- 1 tsp lemon juice
- ⅛ tsp black pepper

Senior Wellness Boost: Rich in omega-3s and heart-healthy fats that support circulation, brain health, and lower cholesterol.

Instructions

1. Spread mashed avocado evenly over toasted whole-grain bread, covering it to the edges for a creamy layer.

2. Top with smoked salmon slices, pressing gently so they stay in place and don't slide off.

3. Drizzle with lemon juice and sprinkle lightly with black pepper for a bright, zesty finish.

4. Serve while it is fresh.

Flavor Tip: Add a citrus twist with orange zest and a drizzle of honey–mustard yogurt.

Cottage Cheese & Pear Bowl

Prep	Cook	Servings
10 min	20 min	2

Nutrition Facts

Calories	180
Protein	14 g
Fiber	3 g
Sodium	220 mg
Fats	2 g
Potassium	210 mg

Ingredients

- ¾ cup low-fat cottage cheese, chilled
- ½ ripe pear, thinly sliced for natural sweetness and soft texture
- 1 tbsp rolled oats or granola
- ¼ tsp ground cinnamon
- ½ tsp honey (optional)

Senior Wellness Boost: A light, protein-powered combination that helps maintain bone density and muscle mass with every serving.

Instructions

1. Spoon the cottage cheese into a small serving bowl, spreading it evenly across the bottom

2. Arrange the pear slices neatly on top of the cottage cheese, then sprinkle with oats or granola.

3. Dust lightly with cinnamon and drizzle a touch of honey over the top for balance.

4. Serve chilled as a refreshing, protein-packed bowl.

Flavor Tip: Sprinkle crushed walnuts or pecans on top to boost flavor.

Cinnamon Rice & Breakfast Bowl

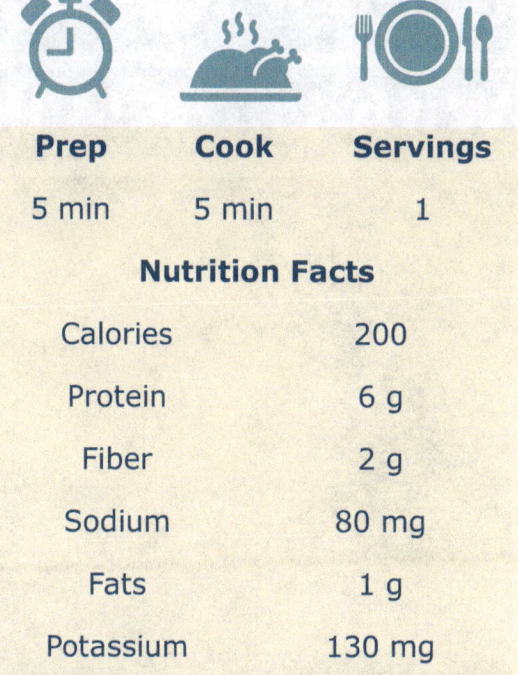

Prep	Cook	Servings
5 min	5 min	1

Nutrition Facts	
Calories	200
Protein	6 g
Fiber	2 g
Sodium	80 mg
Fats	1 g
Potassium	130 mg

Ingredients

- ½ cup cooked rice, cooled slightly
- ½ cup low-fat milk, warmed gently to blend flavors smoothly
- 1 tbsp raisins
- ½ tsp cinnamon
- 1 tsp honey

Senior Wellness Boost: Naturally warming and satisfying; cinnamon supports balanced blood sugar and heart health throughout the day.

Instructions

1. Place the cooked rice and milk in a small saucepan. Warm gently over medium-low heat for 3–4 minutes, and stir until the mixture is creamy.

2. Stir in the cinnamon and raisins, letting the flavors blend into the warm rice.

3. Add a drizzle of honey for gentle sweetness, stirring to combine.

4. Spoon into a bowl and serve warm as a cozy, comforting breakfast.

Flavor Tip: Add sliced banana or a drizzle of warm honey for extra comfort and gentle sweetness with every spoonful.

Golden Turmeric
With Latte Milk

Prep	Cook	Servings
5 min	5 min	1

Nutrition Facts

Calories	120
Protein	3 g
Fiber	2 g
Sodium	90 mg
Fats	1 g
Potassium	200 mg

Ingredients

- 1 cup unsweetened almond milk, warmed gently for a smooth, dairy-free base
- ½ tsp ground turmeric
- ¼ tsp ground cinnamon
- 1 tsp honey (optional)
- Pinch black pepper

Senior Wellness Boost: Turmeric's curcumin helps calm inflammation, soothe joints, and support healthy aging when enjoyed regularly.

Instructions

1. Pour the almond milk into a small saucepan and warm it gently over medium heat.
2. Whisk in the turmeric, cinnamon, and black pepper together.
3. Let the mixture simmer softly for 3–4 minutes, stirring occasionally, until the flavors are well blended.
4. Remove from the heat and, if you prefer a touch of sweetness, stir in the honey.

Flavor Tip: Add a pinch of black pepper or cardamom to boost flavor.

Cheddar Broccoli Egg Cups

Prep	Cook	Servings
6 min	4 min	2

Nutrition Facts	
Calories	170
Protein	12 g
Fiber	2 g
Sodium	230 mg
Fats	2 g
Potassium	210 mg

Ingredients

- 3 eggs
- ½ cup broccoli florets, finely chopped for even cooking and added fiber
- ¼ cup reduced-fat cheddar cheese, freshly shredded for creamy, melted flavor
- 1 tsp olive oil
- ¼ tsp black pepper

Senior Wellness Boost: High in calcium and antioxidants, this combo supports bone strength and immune resilience in older adults.

Instructions

1. Preheat oven to 375°F (190°C) and lightly grease 4 muffin cups.
2. Whisk eggs and black pepper in a bowl until smooth.
3. Stir in chopped broccoli and shredded cheddar.
4. Pour evenly into cups, filling three-quarters full.
5. Bake 12–14 minutes until set and golden.
6. Cool slightly, remove from pan, and serve warm for a quick, protein-rich breakfast.

Flavor Tip: Stir in diced red peppers or green onions before baking.

Cottage Cheese & Pineapple Cups

Prep	Cook	Servings
5 min	3 min	1

Nutrition Facts	
Calories	190
Protein	3 g
Fiber	13 g
Sodium	210 mg
Fats	2 g
Potassium	290 mg

Ingredients

- ¾ cup low-fat cottage cheese, for a warm, aromatic finish
- ½ cup pineapple chunks (fresh or canned, drained)
- 2 tbsp rolled oats, for light crunch and added fiber
- ½ tsp honey (optional)
- Pinch cinnamon, for a warm, aromatic finish

Senior Wellness Boost: Pineapple's natural enzymes promote better digestion, while protein aids recovery and daily energy.

Instructions

1. Place the oats in a dry skillet over medium heat and toast for 2–3 minutes, stirring often, until they turn lightly golden and fragrant.

2. Spoon the cottage cheese into a small cup or bowl, making a smooth base.

3. Add the pineapple chunks on top, then sprinkle with the warm toasted oats for crunch.

4. Finish with a light drizzle of honey and a dusting of cinnamon.

Flavor Tip: Toast the oats in a dry skillet before topping for a nutty aroma and satisfying crunch.

Almond Dates
Energy Bites

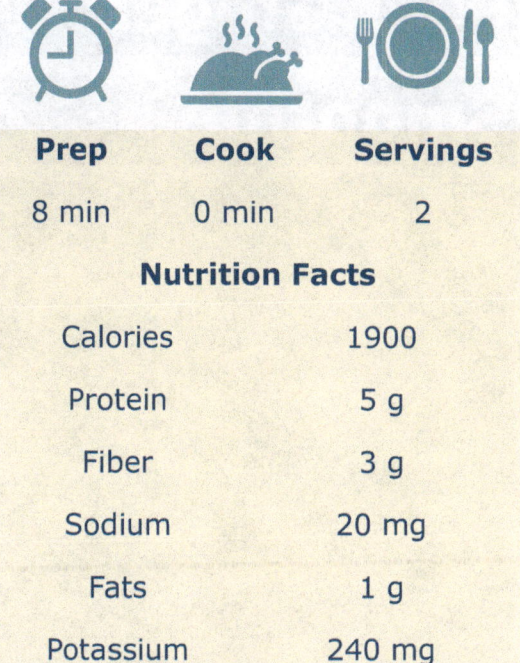

Prep	Cook	Servings
8 min	0 min	2

Nutrition Facts

Calories	1900
Protein	5 g
Fiber	3 g
Sodium	20 mg
Fats	1 g
Potassium	240 mg

Ingredients

- 1 cup pitted dates, soft and sticky for natural sweetness and easy blending
- ½ cup almonds
- ½ cup oats
- ½ tsp cinnamon
- 1 tsp honey, to help bind and enhance natural sweetness

Senior Wellness Boost: A wholesome energy snack that supports heart rhythm, reduces fatigue, and offers natural sweetness without added sugar.

Instructions

1. Place the dates, almonds, oats, cinnamon, and honey in a food processor.

2. Pulse several times until the mixture begins to stick together and forms a soft, crumbly dough.

3. Scoop out small portions and roll them between your palms to form bite-sized balls.

4. Arrange the bites on a plate and chill for about 20 minutes to firm up before serving.

Flavor Tip: Roll in unsweetened coconut or cocoa powder for a fun flavor twist and a rich, treat-like finish.

Pear Ginger Smoothie

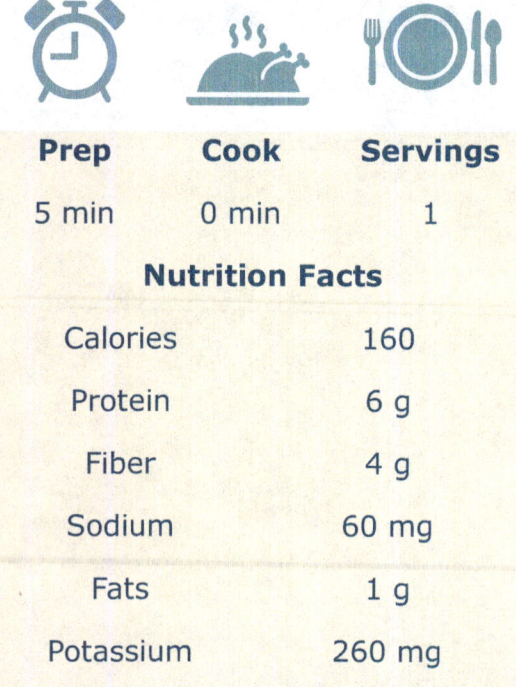

Prep	Cook	Servings
5 min	0 min	1

Nutrition Facts

Calories	160
Protein	6 g
Fiber	4 g
Sodium	60 mg
Fats	1 g
Potassium	260 mg

Ingredients

- 1 ripe pear, chopped into small pieces
- 1 cup low-fat milk (or unsweetened almond milk), for a light, creamy base
- 2 tbsp oats
- ½ tsp fresh ginger, finely grated
- 1 tsp honey

Senior Wellness Boost: Gentle on Digestion, this blend provides antioxidants and fiber to support gut comfort and immune balance.

Instructions

1. Add pear, milk, oats, ginger, and honey to a blender jug, combining well for consistency and balanced flavor throughout.

2. Blend on high speed until smooth and creamy, with no chunks remaining at all, ensuring a silky texture.

3. Pour into a glass and chill briefly if desired for extra refreshment, enhanced flavor, and a naturally energizing finis

4. Enjoy right away for a light, refreshing drink.

Flavor Tip: Add a squeeze of lime juice or a dash of cinnamon.

Comforting Soups & Fresh Salads

Creamy Tomato Basil Soup

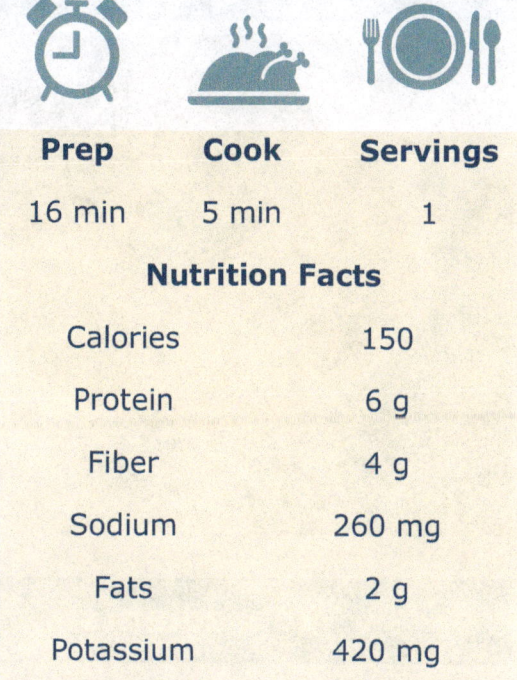

Prep	Cook	Servings
16 min	5 min	1

Nutrition Facts

Calories	150
Protein	6 g
Fiber	4 g
Sodium	260 mg
Fats	2 g
Potassium	420 mg

Ingredients

- 3 cups canned tomatoes
- 1 cup low-sodium vegetable broth
- ½ cup low-fat plain Greek yogurt
- 2 tbsp fresh basil, chopped
- 1 tsp olive oil

Senior Wellness Boost: Tomatoes supports heart health and circulation, while basil promote cell protection.

Instructions

1. Heat olive oil in a pot over medium heat until gently shimmering.
2. Add tomatoes and broth; simmer for 10 minutes until soft and fragrant.
3. Blend until smooth and creamy, reaching a velvety consistency.
4. Stir in yogurt and basil until combined and evenly mixed.
5. Serve warm and fresh for a light, comforting soup.

Flavor Tip: Add pinch of smoked paprika or balsamic vinegar.

Carrot Lentil Soup With Oil Drizzle

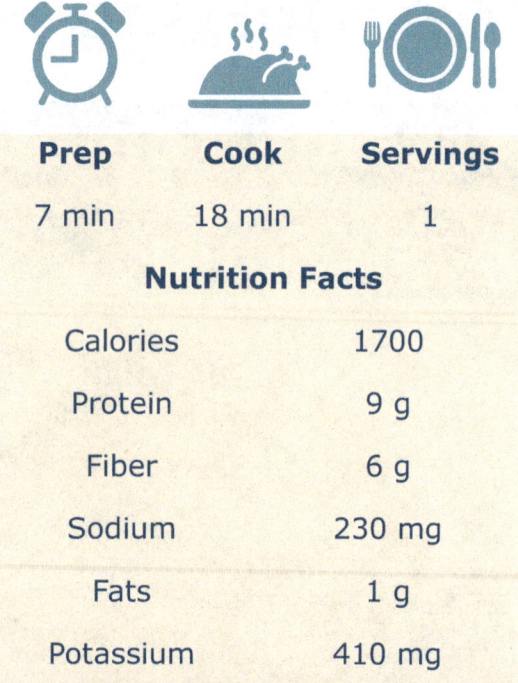

Prep	Cook	Servings
7 min	18 min	1

Nutrition Facts	
Calories	1700
Protein	9 g
Fiber	6 g
Sodium	230 mg
Fats	1 g
Potassium	410 mg

Ingredients

- 1 cup red lentils, rinsed thoroughly
- 2 cups carrots, chopped evenly for natural sweetness
- 3 cups low-sodium vegetable broth, to keep the soup light
- 1 tsp cumin
- 1 tsp olive oil

Senior Wellness Boost: Protein-rich lentils and beta-carotene–packed carrots help maintain vision, reduce cholesterol, and keep energy levels steady.

Instructions

1. In a medium pot, combine the carrots, lentils, broth, and cumin. Stir gently to mix.

2. Bring to a simmer and cook for 15–18 minutes, until the lentils are soft and the carrots are tender.

3. Use a hand blender (or carefully transfer to a blender) to puree the soup until smooth and creamy.

4. Ladle into bowls and finish with a light drizzle of olive oil before serving warm.

Flavor Tip: Stir in ground cumin or coriander for gentle warmth.

Broccoli Soup With Cauli Flower

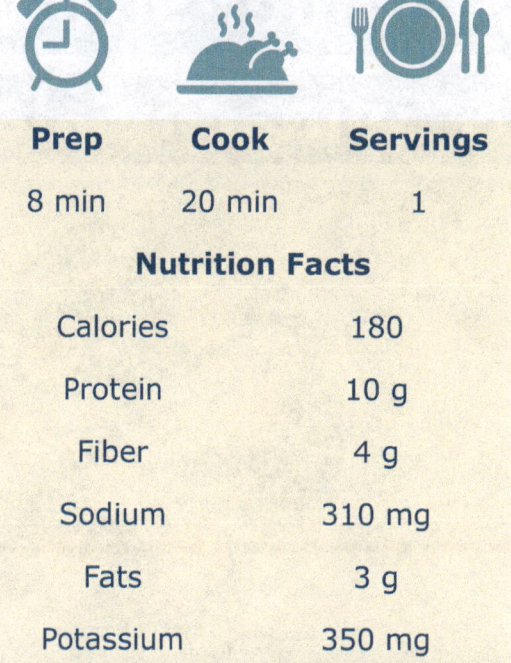

Prep	Cook	Servings
8 min	20 min	1

Nutrition Facts

Calories	180
Protein	10 g
Fiber	4 g
Sodium	310 mg
Fats	3 g
Potassium	350 mg

Ingredients

- 2 cups cauliflower florets
- 1 cup broccoli florets
- 2 cups low-sodium vegetable broth
- ½ cup reduced-fat cheddar cheese, shredded
- 1 tsp olive oil

Senior Wellness Boost: A fiber-filled, low-sodium blend that supports bone health, digestion, and natural detoxification through cruciferous nutrients.

Instructions

1. Heat olive oil in a pot over medium heat. Add cauliflower and broccoli; cook 5 minutes until tender.
2. Pour in broth and simmer 10 minutes until tender and flavors blend beautifully.
3. Blend until smooth and creamy, achieving a rich, velvety texture.
4. Stir in cheddar while hot until melted completely and evenly combined.
5. Ladle into bowls and serve warm.

Flavor Tip: Sprinkle with a pinch of nutmeg or black pepper before serving.

Summer Strawberry & Spinach Salad

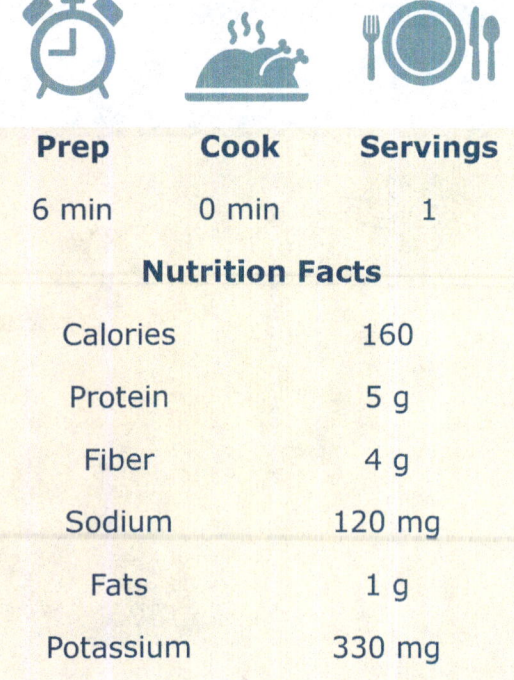

Prep	Cook	Servings
6 min	0 min	1

Nutrition Facts

Calories	160
Protein	5 g
Fiber	4 g
Sodium	120 mg
Fats	1 g
Potassium	330 mg

Ingredients

- 2 cups baby spinach, rinsed and patted dry
- 1 cup strawberries, thinly sliced
- 2 tbsp walnuts, chopped
- 1 tbsp crumbled feta (low-sodium if available)
- 1 tsp balsamic vinegar

Senior Wellness Boost: Strawberries bring antioxidants that protect the heart, while spinach provides iron and potassium for balanced blood pressure.

Instructions

1. Place the fresh spinach leaves into a large serving bowl, spreading them out evenly to create a fresh, colorful base.

2. Add the sliced strawberries, walnuts, and crumbled feta on top of the spinach for a mix of sweetness, crunch, and creaminess.

3. Drizzle lightly with balsamic vinegar for flavor, then toss gently to coat evenly.

4. Chill it for 15 minutes and then serve.

Flavor Tip: Add toasted almonds or a crumble of feta cheese.

Roasted Beet & Walnut Salad

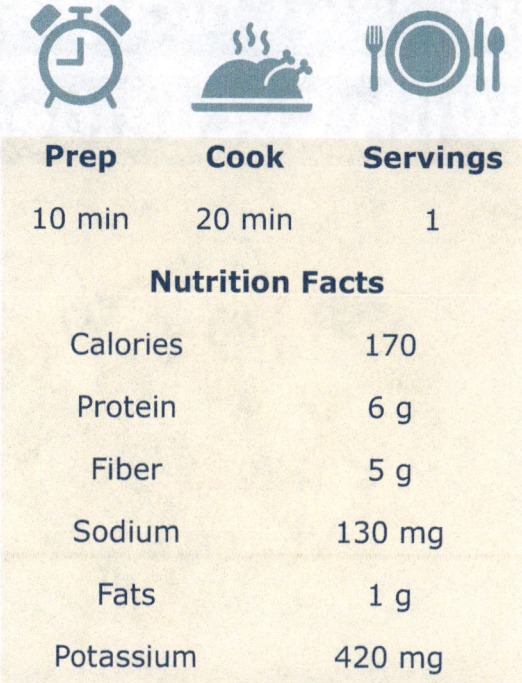

Prep	Cook	Servings
10 min	20 min	1

Nutrition Facts

Calories	170
Protein	6 g
Fiber	5 g
Sodium	130 mg
Fats	1 g
Potassium	420 mg

Ingredients

- 2 medium beets, peeled and cubed
- 2 tbsp walnuts, roughly chopped for crunch
- 2 cups mixed greens, rinsed and dried
- 2 tsp olive oil
- 2 tsp orange juice

Senior Wellness Boost: Beets boost blood flow and stamina, while walnuts offer omega-3s that help reduce inflammation and support brain function.

Instructions

1. Preheat oven to 400°F (200°C). Roast beets on a baking sheet for 20 minutes until tender and slightly caramelized. Cool slightly, then slice thinly.
2. Place mixed greens in a large bowl, spreading them evenly as a base.
3. Add sliced beets and sprinkle with walnuts for a crunchy, nutty contrast.
4. Whisk olive oil and orange juice, drizzle over salad, and toss gently to coat.
5. Serve fresh and bright.

Flavor Tip: Add a drizzle of honey or a few orange zest curls.

Greek Chickpea Salad With Cucumber

Prep	Cook	Servings
7 min	0 min	1

Nutrition Facts

Calories	190
Protein	8 g
Fiber	5 g
Sodium	250 mg
Fats	1 g
Potassium	350 mg

Ingredients

- 1 cup canned chickpeas, rinsed and drained well for a clean, mild taste
- ½ cucumber, diced into small cubes
- 2 tbsp onion, finely diced for a light, zesty bite
- 1 tsp olive oil
- 1 tsp fresh dill, chopped finely

Senior Wellness Boost: Chickpeas add plant protein and fiber for blood sugar control, while cucumber hydrates and aids digestion.

Instructions

1. Combine chickpeas, cucumber, and onion in a medium bowl, mixing gently to combine evenly.
2. Drizzle with olive oil and sprinkle with fresh dill for aroma and freshness.
3. Toss gently until evenly coated and ingredients glisten lightly with dressing.
4. Cover and chill for 10 minutes to let the flavors blend beautifully.
5. Serve cool for a light, refreshing salad with crisp texture, herby flavor, and balanced taste.

Flavor Tip: Add a squeeze of lemon and a few crumbles of feta.

Quinoa Kale Bowl With Vinaigrette

Prep	Cook	Servings
8 min	15 min	1

Nutrition Facts

Calories	200
Protein	7 g
Fiber	5 g
Sodium	180 mg
Fats	1 g
Potassium	360 mg

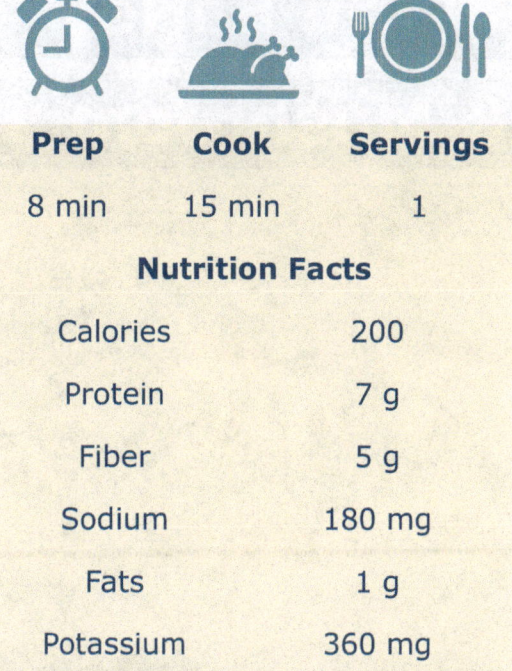

Ingredients

- ½ cup cooked quinoa, cooled and fluffed
- 1 cup kale, chopped finely for tenderness
- ¼ cup cherry tomatoes, halved
- 1 tsp olive oil
- 2 tsp lemon juice

Senior Wellness Boost: Quinoa delivers complete protein, and kale's calcium and antioxidants promote strong bones and heart wellness.

Instructions

1. Place the cooked quinoa and fresh kale into a medium serving bowl, mixing them lightly.

2. Add the halved cherry tomatoes on top for color and freshness.

3. In a small cup, whisk together the olive oil and lemon juice until smooth.

4. Drizzle the dressing over the bowl, then toss gently until everything is evenly coated.

5. Serve slightly warm and enjoy.

Flavor Tip: Add diced avocado or a sprinkle of sunflower seeds on top.

Warm Barley & Mushroom Salad

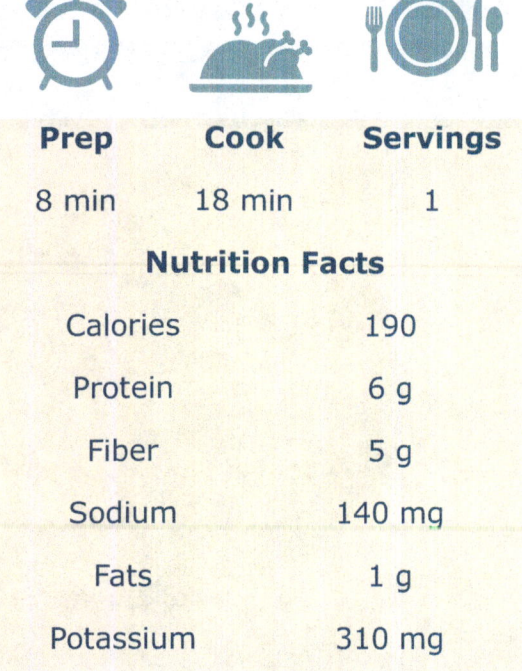

Prep	Cook	Servings
8 min	18 min	1

Nutrition Facts	
Calories	190
Protein	6 g
Fiber	5 g
Sodium	140 mg
Fats	1 g
Potassium	310 mg

Ingredients

- ½ cup pearl barley, cooked until tender and slightly chewy
- 1 cup mushrooms, thinly sliced for earthy flavor and savory depth
- 1 cup spinach, chopped
- 1 tsp olive oil
- 1 tsp lemon juice

Senior Wellness Boost: Barley's soluble fiber supports cholesterol balance, while mushrooms add immune-boosting nutrients for daily vitality.

Instructions

1. Cook barley according to package directions until tender, then drain and set aside.

2. Heat olive oil in a skillet over medium heat. Add mushrooms and sauté 5 minutes until golden.

3. Stir in spinach and cook 1–2 minutes until wilted.

4. Combine with barley, drizzle with lemon juice, and toss properly.

5. Serve as a warm wholesome plate and enjoy.

Flavor Tip: Stir in a touch of soy sauce or a few drops of truffle oil.

Brown Rice & Pepper Bowl

Prep	Cook	Servings
6 min	18 min	1

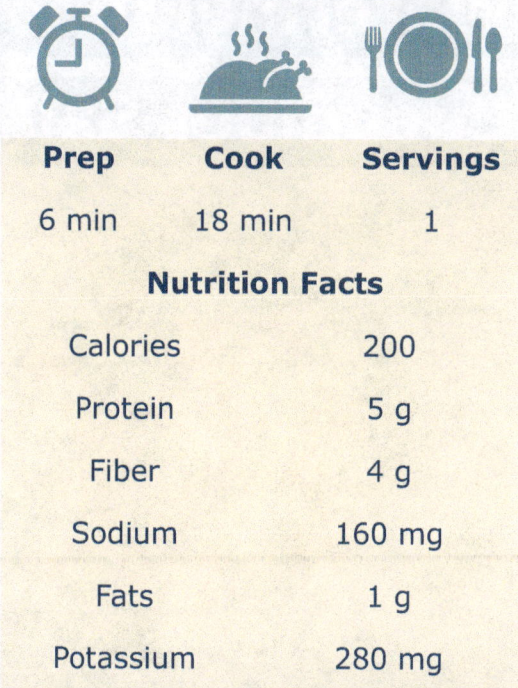

Nutrition Facts

Calories	200
Protein	5 g
Fiber	4 g
Sodium	160 mg
Fats	1 g
Potassium	280 mg

Ingredients

- ½ cup cooked brown rice, cooled and fluffed
- ½ cup roasted red bell peppers, sliced thin for smoky sweetness and color
- ½ cup zucchini, sliced and lightly sautéed
- 1 tsp olive oil
- 1 tsp balsamic vinegar

Senior Wellness Boost: Whole-grain brown rice stabilizes energy, and peppers provide vitamin C to strengthen immunity and reduce stress.

Instructions

1. Preheat the oven to 400°F (200°C). Place the zucchini and bell peppers on a baking sheet and roast for about 15 minutes, or until tender and lightly browned.

2. Place the cooked rice in a medium serving bowl, and top them with the roasted vegetables, arranging them neatly.

3. Drizzle with olive oil and a splash of balsamic vinegar for flavor. Serve warm as a colorful, wholesome bowl.

Flavor Tip: Add a squeeze of lime or a few fresh cilantro leaves on top

Watermelon Cucumber Salad

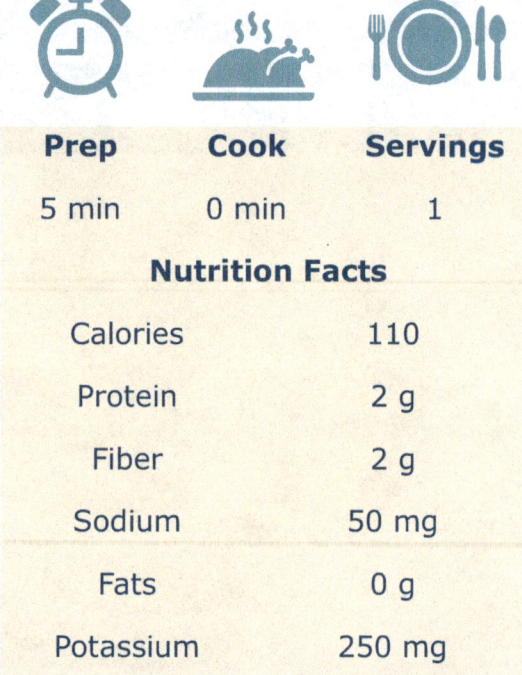

Prep	Cook	Servings
5 min	0 min	1

Nutrition Facts	
Calories	110
Protein	2 g
Fiber	2 g
Sodium	50 mg
Fats	0 g
Potassium	250 mg

Ingredients

- 1 cup watermelon, cubed
- ½ cucumber, diced finely for a crisp, cooling contrast
- 1 tbsp fresh mint, chopped to release its refreshing aroma
- 1 tsp lime juice
- Pinch black pepper

Senior Wellness Boost: Naturally hydrating and rich in potassium, this combo helps regulate blood pressure and soothe inflammation.

Instructions

1. In a bowl, combine diced watermelon and sliced cucumber for a refreshing base.
2. Add chopped mint leaves and crumbled feta cheese for flavor contrast.
3. Drizzle with olive oil and a splash of lime juice.
4. Toss gently and chill 10 minutes before serving cool and crisp. Enjoy your watermelon cucumber salad.

Flavor Tip: Add a squeeze of lime or a few fresh cilantro leaves on top to enhance flavor.

Tuna & White Bean Salad

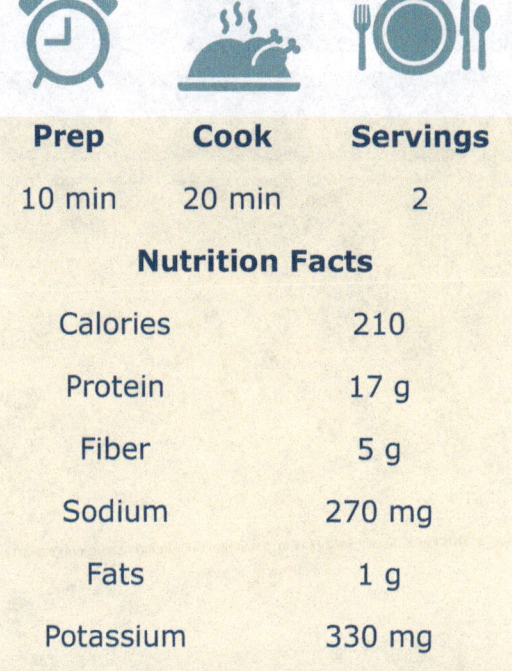

Prep	Cook	Servings
10 min	20 min	2

Nutrition Facts

Calories	210
Protein	17 g
Fiber	5 g
Sodium	270 mg
Fats	1 g
Potassium	330 mg

Ingredients

- 1 can tuna (low-sodium, drained)
- ½ cup white beans, rinsed and drained
- ¼ cup cucumber, diced
- 1 tsp olive oil
- 1 tbsp parsley, chopped

Senior Wellness Boost: Omega-3s from tuna and fiber from beans support heart health, brain function, and healthy cholesterol levels.

Instructions

1. Place the tuna, beans, and cucumber together in a medium mixing bowl. Break the tuna into small pieces with a fork so it blends evenly.

2. Drizzle with olive oil and sprinkle with fresh parsley.

3. Toss everything gently until the ingredients are well coated.

4. Serve chilled straight from the refrigerator or at room temperature for a light, protein-rich salad.

Flavor Tip: Add a splash of red wine vinegar or lemon juice to highlight the tuna's flavor and make the beans taste lighter.

Cabbage Carrot Slaw & Yoghurt Dressing

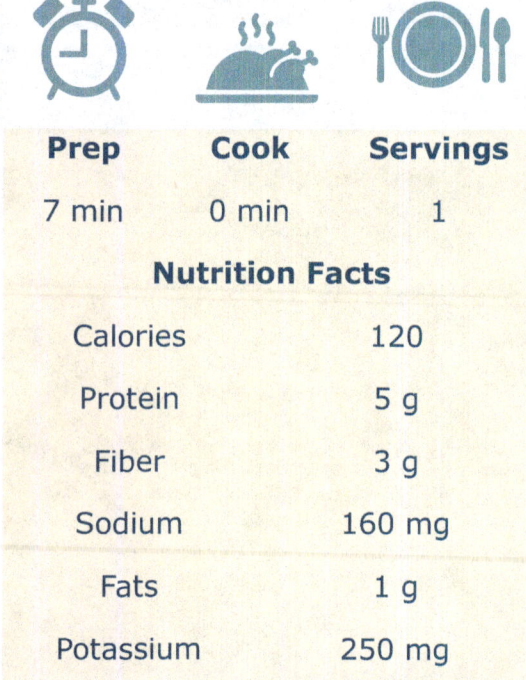

Prep	Cook	Servings
7 min	0 min	1

Nutrition Facts

Calories	120
Protein	5 g
Fiber	3 g
Sodium	160 mg
Fats	1 g
Potassium	250 mg

Ingredients

- 2 cups green cabbage, shredded
- 1 cup carrot, shredded
- ½ cup low-fat plain Greek yogurt
- 1 tsp lemon juice for a zesty flavor
- ¼ tsp black pepper

Senior Wellness Boost: Crunchy cabbage aids digestion and gut health, while yogurt offers calcium and probiotics for strong bones and immunity and keeps you healthy and fit.

Instructions

1. Place the shredded cabbage and carrots together in a large serving bowl.

2. In a smaller bowl, whisk the yogurt, lemon juice, and black pepper until smooth and creamy.

3. Pour the dressing over the cabbage and carrots.

4. Toss well until the vegetables are evenly coated

5. Chill it for 15 minutes and then serve as a crisp, refreshing side.

Flavor Tip: Mix a teaspoon of apple cider vinegar to enhance flavor.

Sweet Corn & Potato Cheddar

	Prep	Cook	Servings
	8 min	20 min	1

Nutrition Facts

Calories	190
Protein	6 g
Fiber	4 g
Sodium	240 mg
Fats	2 g
Potassium	400 mg

Ingredients

- 2 cups low-sodium vegetable broth
- 1 cup corn kernels (fresh or frozen)
- 1 cup potato, diced finely diced finely for creamy thickness and comfort
- ½ cup low-fat milk
- 1 tsp olive oil

Senior Wellness Boost: A satisfying, potassium-rich mix that supports nerve function, blood pressure balance, and energy replenishment.

Instructions

1. Heat olive oil in a pot over medium heat. Add diced potatoes and cook 5 minutes, stirring until slightly softened.

2. Add broth and corn, simmer 12–15 minutes until potatoes are tender.

3. Stir in milk for creaminess and ensure it reaches the right thickness.

4. Blend half the soup for texture, then stir to combine. Serve while it is warm to enjoy a hearty comforting soup.

Flavor Tip: Add smoked paprika or chopped chives to add warmth.

Roasted Zucchini & Tomato Salad

Prep	Cook	Servings
6 min	15 min	1

Nutrition Facts	
Calories	140
Protein	4 g
Fiber	3 g
Sodium	150 mg
Fats	1 g
Potassium	320 mg

Ingredients

- 1 cup zucchini, sliced into thin rounds for a tender, lightly crisp texture

- 1 cup cherry tomatoes, halved for juicy sweetness and vibrant color

- 1 tsp olive oil

- 1 tsp balsamic vinegar

- 1 tbsp fresh basil, chopped

Senior Wellness Boost: Zucchini and tomato pair for antioxidant protection, helping reduce inflammation and support eye and heart health.

Instructions

1. Preheat oven to 400°F (200°C) and line a baking sheet with parchment paper.

2. Slice zucchini into half-moons and cherry tomatoes in half; toss with olive oil.

3. Spread evenly on the sheet and roast 15 minutes until zucchini is golden and tomatoes soft.

4. Transfer to a bowl, drizzle with balsamic vinegar, sprinkle basil, and toss gently. Serve while it is warm.

Flavor Tip: Add a crumble of goat cheese or drizzle of pesto.

Apple Walnut Kale Slaw

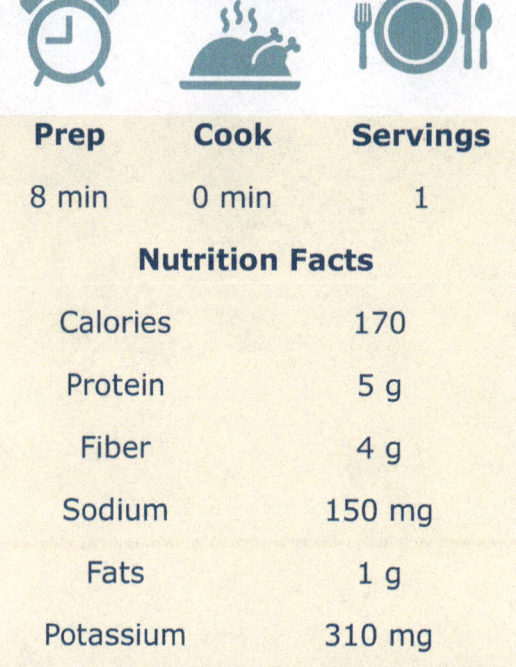

Prep	Cook	Servings
8 min	0 min	1

Nutrition Facts	
Calories	170
Protein	5 g
Fiber	4 g
Sodium	150 mg
Fats	1 g
Potassium	310 mg

Ingredients

- 2 cups kale, shredded finely for easy chewing
- 1 apple, thinly sliced for crisp texture and natural sweetness
- 2 tbsp walnuts, chopped for added crunch
- 1 tsp olive oil
- 1 tsp lemon juice

Senior Wellness Boost: Apples and kale promote heart and digestive health, while walnuts supply omega-3s for sharper memory and focus.

Instructions

1. Rinse and dry the kale, then tear it into bite-sized pieces. Place the kale and thin apple slices into a large salad bowl.

2. Add the walnuts on top for crunch and flavor.

3. In a small cup, whisk together olive oil and fresh lemon juice until smooth. Drizzle this dressing evenly over the salad.

4. Gently toss everything together so the kale is coated and the apples glisten. Serve fresh and crisp and enjoy.

Flavor Tip: Toss in a few dried cranberries or a drizzle of honey for a sweet-tart contrast that enhances the nutty crunch and crisp kale.

Wholesome Mains

Lemon Baked COD With Spinach

Prep	Cook	Servings
6 min	14 min	1

Nutrition Facts

Calories	190
Protein	25 g
Fiber	2 g
Sodium	230 mg
Fats	1 g
Potassium	430 mg

Ingredients

- 1 cod fillet (4 oz), rinsed and patted dry
- 1 cup fresh spinach
- 1 tsp olive oil
- 1 garlic clove, minced
- 2 tsp lemon juice

Senior Wellness Boost: Lean protein from cod supports heart and muscle health, while spinach improve circulation and bones.

Instructions

1. Preheat oven to 375°F (190°C) and lightly oil a small baking dish.

2. Place cod fillet inside, drizzle with olive oil and fresh lemon juice.

3. Sprinkle evenly with minced garlic. Bake 12–14 minutes until opaque and flaky.

4. Serve over fresh spinach, and cracked pepper with lemon.

Flavor Tip: Add a sprinkle of fresh parsley or dill before serving.

Chicken with Rosemary

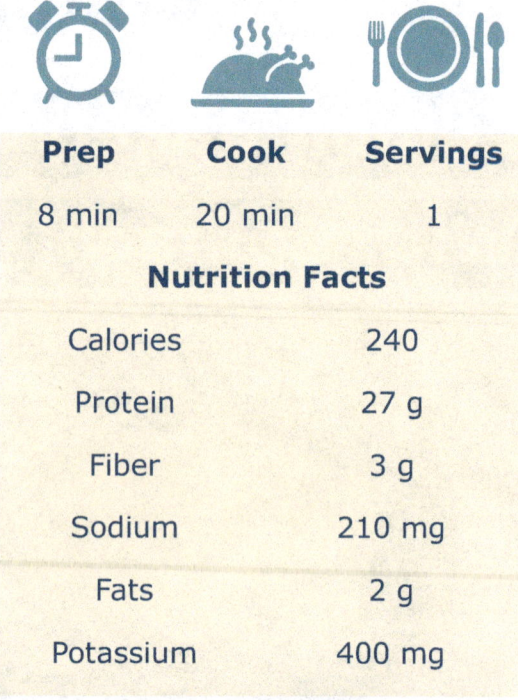

Prep	Cook	Servings
8 min	20 min	1

Nutrition Facts

Calories	240
Protein	27 g
Fiber	3 g
Sodium	210 mg
Fats	2 g
Potassium	400 mg

Ingredients

- 1 chicken breast (4 oz), trimmed and patted dry for even cooking
- 1 apple, sliced finely to enhance flavor
- 1 tsp olive oil
- 1 tsp fresh rosemary
- ¼ tsp black pepper

Senior Wellness Boost: Tender chicken provides essential protein, and rosemary's antioxidants support memory and overall immune wellness.

Instructions

1. Heat olive oil in a skillet over medium heat until gently shimmering.

2. Add chicken breast, season with rosemary and black pepper, and cook about 6 minutes until golden

3. Add apple slices during the last 5 minutes and let them soften.

4. Continue cooking until chicken reaches 165°F and apples turn tender and golden brown.

5. Serve warm for a sweet, savory, and aromatic dish.

Flavor Tip: Sprinkle a splash of apple cider or white wine on the pan.

Turkey Tomato Skillet

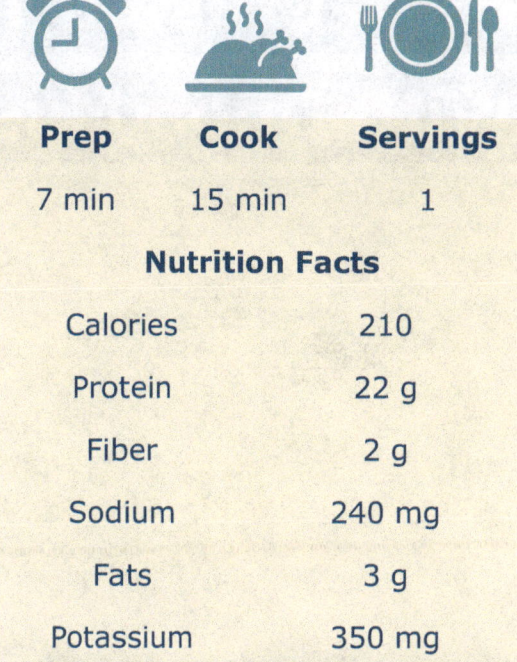

Prep	Cook	Servings
7 min	15 min	1

Nutrition Facts

Calories	210
Protein	22 g
Fiber	2 g
Sodium	240 mg
Fats	3 g
Potassium	350 mg

Ingredients

- ½ lb. ground turkey
- 1 cup diced tomatoes (no-salt-added), for natural sweetness and rich flavor
- ¼ cup onion, finely diced for mild aroma and depth
- 1 tsp olive oil
- ½ tsp oregano

Senior Wellness Boost: Turkey offers lean protein for muscle maintenance, while tomatoes provide lycopene to protect heart and eye health.

Instructions

1. Heat olive oil in a skillet over medium heat. Add onion and cook about 3 minutes until softened.
2. Stir in ground turkey and cook 6 minutes, breaking it apart with a spoon, until browned.
3. Add diced tomatoes and oregano, stirring to combine.
4. Reduce heat slightly and simmer 6 minutes, allowing the flavors to blend and sauce to thicken.
5. Serve warm and enjoy.

Flavor Tip: Stir in a pinch of smoked paprika or chili flakes for gentle warmth that deepens the tomato base and adds Mediterranean flair.

Herb Crusted Tilapia With Dijon Mustard

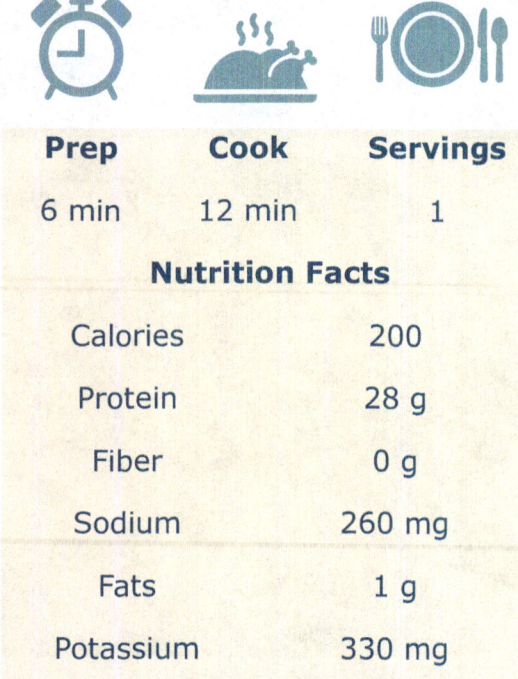

Prep	Cook	Servings
6 min	12 min	1

Nutrition Facts

Calories	200
Protein	28 g
Fiber	0 g
Sodium	260 mg
Fats	1 g
Potassium	330 mg

Ingredients

- 1 tilapia fillet (4 oz), rinsed and patted dry for a light, flaky base
- 1 tsp Dijon mustard
- 1 tbsp breadcrumbs (whole wheat if available)
- ½ tsp dried parsley
- 1 tsp olive oil

Senior Wellness Boost: Tilapia's light protein aids muscle recovery, and mustard's antioxidants promote circulation and healthy cholesterol levels.

Instructions

1. Preheat oven to 375°F (190°C) and line a baking sheet with parchment paper.

2. Place tilapia fillets on the sheet and brush each lightly with Dijon mustard to coat.

3. In a small bowl, mix breadcrumbs with chopped parsley. Sprinkle the mixture evenly over the fish.

4. Drizzle a little olive oil on top to help the crust crisp.

5. Bake for about 12 minutes until the top is golden. Serve warm.

Flavor Tip: Squeeze fresh lemon over the fillets right before serving.

Chicken Bake With Olives

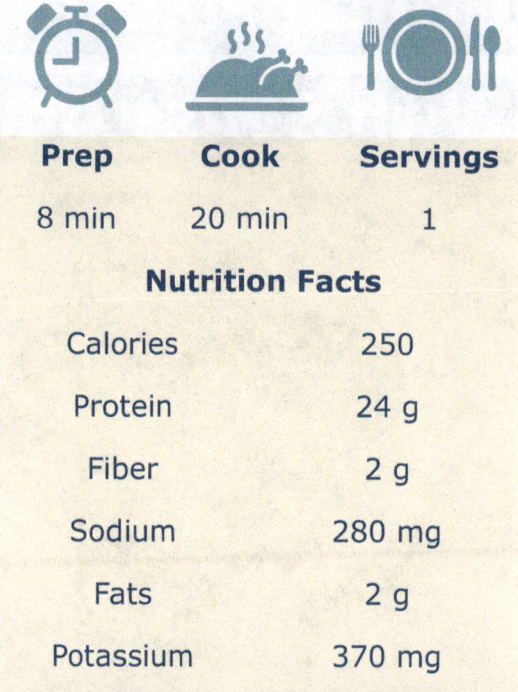

Prep	Cook	Servings
8 min	20 min	1

Nutrition Facts

Calories	250
Protein	24 g
Fiber	2 g
Sodium	280 mg
Fats	2 g
Potassium	370 mg

Ingredients

- 1 chicken thigh, trimmed for tenderness and lower fat content
- ½ cup diced tomatoes (no-salt-added)
- 2 tbsp black olives, sliced
- 1 tsp olive oil
- ½ tsp dried oregano

Senior Wellness Boost: Olives and olive oil provide heart-healthy fats that reduce inflammation and support balanced blood pressure.

Instructions

1. Preheat oven to 375°F. Place chicken breasts in a lightly oiled baking dish.

2. Add cherry tomatoes, sliced olives, and minced garlic on top.

3. Drizzle with olive oil, sprinkle oregano, and season with black pepper.

4. Bake 25–30 minutes until golden and chicken reaches 165°F, juicy and tender.

5. Enjoy while it is warm.

Flavor Tip: Add a handful of fresh basil or oregano after baking to enhance the flavor of the ingredients.

Grilled Mackerel With Swiss Chard

Prep	Cook	Servings
7 min	12 min	1

Nutrition Facts	
Calories	230
Protein	26 g
Fiber	3 g
Sodium	200 mg
Fats	2 g
Potassium	440 mg

Ingredients

- 1 mackerel fillet (4 oz)
- 1 cup Swiss chard, chopped for tender greens
- 1 tsp olive oil
- ¼ tsp black pepper
- ½ tsp freshly grated lemon zest, for a bright, citrusy finish

Senior Wellness Boost: Omega-3s from mackerel strengthen heart and brain function, while Swiss chard adds potassium and vitamin K for bone support.

Instructions

1. Heat an outdoor grill or stovetop grill pan to medium heat.

2. Brush mackerel fillets lightly with olive oil, then sprinkle with lemon zest and black pepper.

3. Grill for 4–5 minutes per side, until the fish is opaque and flakes easily with a fork.

4. While the fish cooks, warm ½ teaspoon olive oil in a skillet. Add chopped Swiss chard and sauté 3–4 minutes until just wilted.

Flavor Tip: Finish with a drizzle of olive oil and a squeeze of lemon for a clean, zesty contrast to the fish's rich, smoky flavor.

Simple Lentil Sweet Potato Bowl

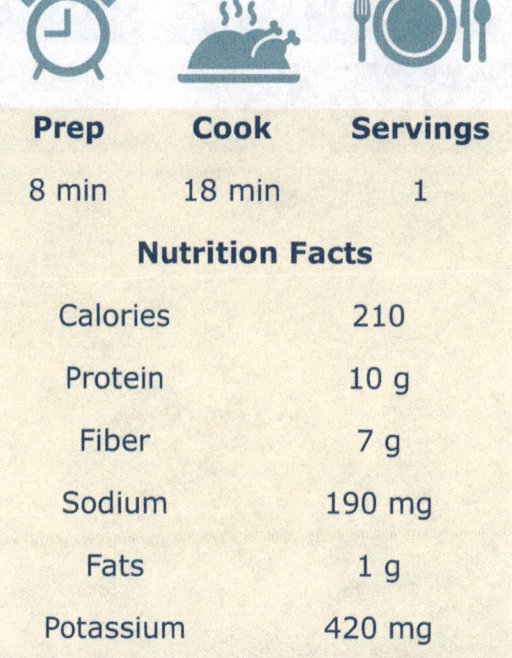

Prep	Cook	Servings
8 min	18 min	1

Nutrition Facts

Calories	210
Protein	10 g
Fiber	7 g
Sodium	190 mg
Fats	1 g
Potassium	420 mg

Ingredients

- 1 cup cooked lentils, drained and tender
- ½ cup sweet potato, cubed into small pieces
- ½ cup onion, diced finely for mild flavor and aroma
- 1 tsp olive oil
- ½ tsp cumin

Senior Wellness Boost: Fiber-rich lentils and sweet potatoes help manage cholesterol, promote digestion, and stabilize energy levels.

Instructions

1. Heat olive oil in a medium skillet over medium heat. Add chopped onion and diced sweet potato, cooking for about 8 minutes, stirring occasionally, until the onion softens and the potatoes begin to brown.

2. Stir in the lentils and sprinkle with cumin for flavor.

3. Continue cooking 5–6 minutes, until the sweet potatoes are tender and the lentils are heated through. Serve warm in a bowl.

Flavor Tip: Stir in a dash of cumin or curry powder for extra warmth and depth to boost flavor.

Pumpkin Red Lentil Stew

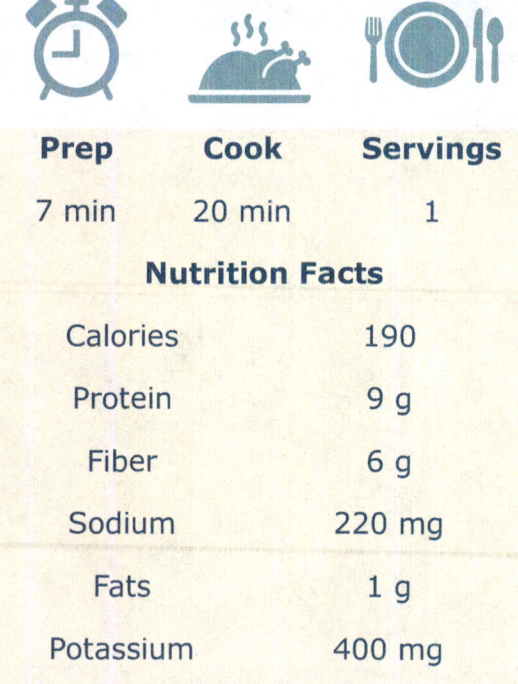

Prep	Cook	Servings
7 min	20 min	1

Nutrition Facts

Calories	190
Protein	9 g
Fiber	6 g
Sodium	220 mg
Fats	1 g
Potassium	400 mg

Ingredients

- 1 cup pumpkin, cubed into small pieces
- ½ cup red lentils, rinsed well for quick cooking
- 2 cups low-sodium vegetable broth
- 1 tsp olive oil
- ½ tsp cumin

Senior Wellness Boost: Beta-carotene–rich pumpkin and protein-packed lentils support immunity, eye health, and steady blood pressure.

Instructions

1. Heat olive oil in a large pot over medium heat. Add the diced pumpkin and cook for about 5 minutes, stirring occasionally, until it begins to soften.

2. Stir in the lentils, vegetable broth, and cumin, mixing well so the flavors combine.

3. Bring to a gentle simmer and cook for about 15 minutes, or until both pumpkin and lentils are tender.

4. Serve warm in bowls as a hearty, comforting stew.

Flavor Tip: Add a swirl of coconut milk or a pinch of cinnamon before serving to make it extra creamy and subtly spiced.

Shrimp Stir-Fry with Snap Peas & Carrots

Prep	Cook	Servings
6 min	10 min	1

Nutrition Facts	
Calories	200
Protein	22 g
Fiber	3 g
Sodium	260 mg
Fats	1 g
Potassium	310 mg

Ingredients

- ½ lb. shrimp, peeled and deveined
- 1 cup snap peas, trimmed for a crisp, fresh crunch
- ½ cup carrots, thinly sliced for natural sweetness
- 1 tsp olive oil
- 1 tsp low-sodium soy sauce

Senior Wellness Boost: Shrimp delivers lean protein and selenium, while colorful vegetables offer antioxidants that aid joint and heart health.

Instructions

1. Heat olive oil in a large skillet or wok over medium-high heat.

2. Add the shrimp in a single layer and cook for 2–3 minutes, until they turn pink and opaque.

3. Add the snap peas and sliced carrots. Stir-fry for about 5 minutes, keeping the vegetables crisp-tender.

4. Splash lightly with low-sodium soy sauce and toss well to coat.

5. Serve and enjoy while it is warm.

Flavor Tip: Add a splash of lime juice or sesame oil at the end.

Cauliflower Mash With Pasta

Prep	Cook	Servings
8 min	15 min	1

Nutrition Facts

Calories	210
Protein	8 g
Fiber	5 g
Sodium	200 mg
Fats	1 g
Potassium	380 mg

Ingredients

- 2 cups cauliflower florets chopped into small pieces
- 1 garlic clove, minced finely
- 1 cup whole-grain pasta, cooked
- ½ cup low-fat milk
- 1 tsp olive oil

Senior Wellness Boost: Cauliflower adds fiber and B vitamins for digestion and energy, making a light, heart-friendly comfort meal.

Instructions

1. Steam cauliflower florets for 8–10 minutes, until very soft and easy to pierce with a fork.

2. Transfer to a blender or food processor. Add garlic, a splash of milk, and olive oil. Blend until smooth and creamy.

3. While still hot, toss the cauliflower mash with freshly cooked pasta, coating the noodles evenly.

4. Serve warm and enjoy!

Flavor Tip: Mix in a spoonful of grated Parmesan or roasted garlic for extra creaminess and a savory kick that complements the mild cauliflower.

Mushroom Asparagus Rice Skillet

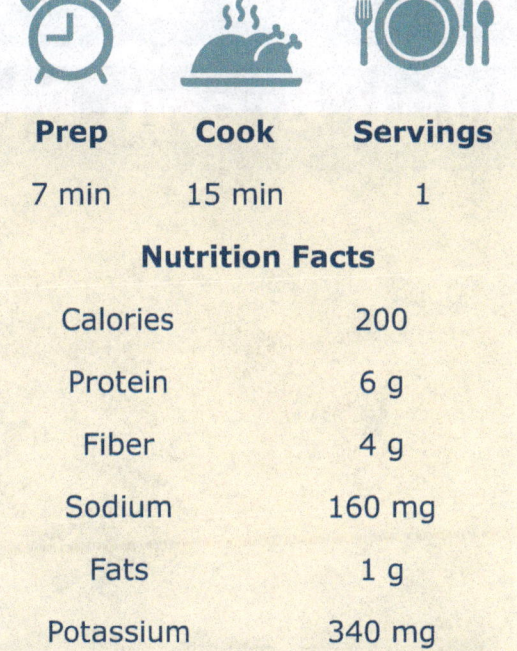

Prep	Cook	Servings
7 min	15 min	1

Nutrition Facts

Calories	200
Protein	6 g
Fiber	4 g
Sodium	160 mg
Fats	1 g
Potassium	340 mg

Ingredients

- ½ cup cooked brown rice, cooled and fluffed
- 1 cup mushrooms, sliced thin for earthy flavor
- ½ cup asparagus, cut into bite-sized pieces
- 1 tsp olive oil
- ¼ tsp black pepper

Senior Wellness Boost: Mushrooms boost immunity with natural vitamin D, and asparagus supports kidney function and blood pressure balance.

Instructions

1. Heat olive oil in a large skillet over medium heat. Add sliced mushrooms and trimmed asparagus pieces.

2. Cook for 6–7 minutes, stirring occasionally, until everything sets well.

3. Stir in the cooked brown rice and season lightly with black pepper.

4. Continue cooking for about 3 minutes, stirring well, until the rice is heated through and flavors blend.

Flavor Tip: Stir in a dash of soy sauce or balsamic vinegar for a rich umami flavor.

Roasted Bell Peppers With Brown Rice

Prep	Cook	Servings
8 min	18 min	1

Nutrition Facts

Calories	220
Protein	14 g
Fiber	17 g
Sodium	3 mg
Fats	1 g
Potassium	170 mg

Ingredients

- 2 bell peppers, halved and seeded for color
- ½ cup cooked brown rice
- ¼ cup onion, diced finely for sweetness
- 1 tsp olive oil
- 1 tbsp parsley, chopped for a bright, herbaceous finish

Senior Wellness Boost: High in fiber and vitamin C, this dish supports digestion and strengthens the immune system naturally.

Instructions

1. Preheat oven to 375°F (190°C). Place bell peppers on a baking sheet, drizzle lightly with olive oil, and roast for about 15 minutes until softened.

2. While the peppers roast, heat a small skillet with a little olive oil. Add chopped onion and cook for about 3 minutes until softened and fragrant.

3. Mix the sautéed onion with cooked rice and fresh parsley and spoon this mixture into the roasted peppers. Serve warm.

Flavor Tip: Add a sprinkle of feta or a drizzle of pesto to boost flavor.

Turkey Meatballs With Tomato-Basil

Prep	Cook	Servings
10 min	18 min	3

Nutrition Facts

Calories	220
Protein	23 g
Fiber	2 g
Sodium	260 mg
Fats	2 g
Potassium	330 mg

Ingredients

- ½ lb. ground turkey, lean and fresh
- 1 cup no-salt tomato sauce for a flavorful base
- 1 tsp dried basil, to add classic Italian aroma and taste
- 1 tsp olive oil to sauté for a rich flavor
- ½ tsp garlic powder

Senior Wellness Boost: Lean turkey and lycopene promote heart health and reduce oxidative stress.

Instructions

1. In a bowl, mix ground turkey with garlic powder. Shape the mixture into small, even-sized meatballs.

2. Heat olive oil in a skillet over medium heat. Add the meatballs and cook for about 6 minutes, turning to brown on all sides.

3. Pour in tomato sauce and add fresh or dried basil. Stir gently to coat the meatballs.

4. Simmer for 10–12 minutes. Serve warm and enjoy.

Flavor Tip: Add a pinch of red pepper flakes or a few fresh basil leaves.

Grilled Eggplant With Mozzarella

Prep	Cook	Servings
6 min	12 min	3

Nutrition Facts

Calories	200
Protein	10 g
Fiber	3 g
Sodium	210 mg
Fats	3 g
Potassium	360 mg

Ingredients

- 1 small eggplant, sliced into even rounds.
- ¼ cup reduced-fat mozzarella, freshly shredded for creamy, melted texture
- 1 tsp olive oil
- ½ tsp dried basil
- ¼ tsp black pepper, to season gently

Senior Wellness Boost: Eggplant's fiber supports gut health, while mozzarella provides calcium and protein for strong bones and muscles.

Instructions

1. Brush both sides of the eggplant slices lightly with olive oil. Season with dried basil and a little black pepper.

2. Arrange the slices on a grill pan or baking sheet. Grill or roast at 400°F (200°C) for about 10 minutes, until tender and golden.

3. Sprinkle each slice with shredded mozzarella.

4. Return to the grill or oven for 2 minutes, just until the cheese melts and bubbles. Serve warm.

Flavor Tip: Drizzle with balsamic glaze or scatter fresh basil over top.

Garlic Herb Trout With Lemon

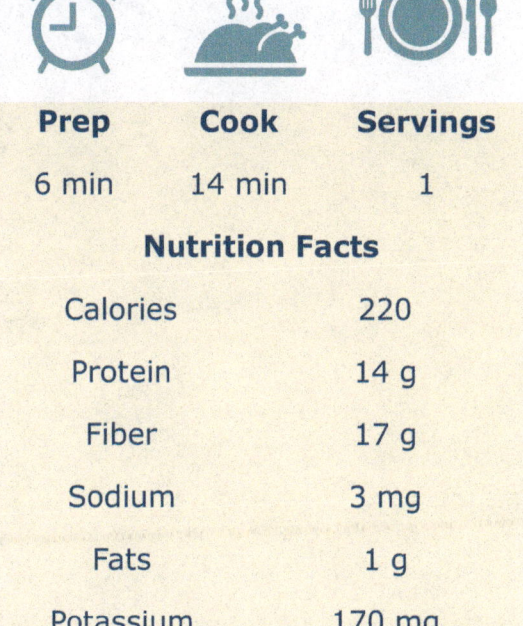

Prep	Cook	Servings
6 min	14 min	1

Nutrition Facts

Calories	220
Protein	14 g
Fiber	17 g
Sodium	3 mg
Fats	1 g
Potassium	170 mg

Ingredients

- 1 trout fillet (4 oz), rinsed and patted dry for delicate, flaky texture
- 1 tsp olive oil
- 1 garlic clove, minced finely
- 1 tsp fresh parsley, chopped
- 2 tsp lemon juice

Senior Wellness Boost: Trout's omega-3s improve heart rhythm, while garlic and lemon enhance immunity and circulation naturally.

Instructions

1. Preheat oven to 375°F (190°C). Lightly oil or line a small baking dish for easy cleanup.

2. Place trout fillets in the dish and drizzle with olive oil and fresh lemon juice to keep them moist.

3. Sprinkle minced garlic and chopped parsley evenly over the top.

4. Serve and enjoy while it is warm.

Flavor Tip: Finish with a pat of olive oil or a sprinkle of fresh thyme to enhance the citrusy, herbed aroma and add richness.

Gentle Drinks & Infusions

Watermelon–Mint Infusion

Prep	Cook	Servings
5 min	0 min	4

Nutrition (per serving): 25 cal. 0 g protein. 1 g fiber. 5 mg sodium

Ingredients

- 1 cup watermelon cubes
- 6 fresh mint leaves
- 4 cups cool water

Flavor Twist: Add cucumber or lime for a crisp twist and refreshing summer flavor.

Instructions

1. Add watermelon and mint to pitcher with water.
2. Chill 20 min. and serve cold, with ice if desired.

Warm Lemon–Honey Water

Prep	Cook	Servings
2 min	2 min	2

Nutrition (per serving): 45 cal · 0 g protein · 0 g fiber · 5 mg sodium

Ingredients

- 2 cups warm water
- 2 lemon slices
- 1 tsp honey

Flavor Twist: Stir in ginger or turmeric for gentle warmth and immune support.

Instructions

1. Heat water until warm.
2. Stir in lemon and honey.
3. Sip slowly while warm.

Almond Milk Golden Latte

Prep	Cook	Servings
10 min	20 min	2

Nutrition (per serving): 120 cal · 3 g protein · 2 g fiber · 95 mg sodium

Ingredients

- 2 cups almond milk
- 1 tsp turmeric
- ½ tsp cinnamon
- 1 tsp honey (optional)
- Pinch black pepper

Flavor Twist: Blend with coconut milk and sprinkle nutmeg for creamy, aromatic comfort.

Instructions

1. Heat almond milk until warm.
2. Whisk in turmeric, cinnamon, and pepper.
3. Simmer 3–4 min; sweeten lightly.

Hibiscus–Berry Iced Tea

Prep	Cook	Servings
5 min	5 min	4

Nutrition (per serving): 40 cal · 0 g protein · 1 g fiber · 0 mg sodium

Ingredients

- 2 hibiscus tea bags
- 1 cup mixed berries
- 1 tsp honey (optional)
- 4 cups water

Flavor Twist: Add orange slices or sparkling water for a fruity, uplifting sip.

Instructions

1. Steep tea bags in hot water 5 min.
2. Stir in berries; chill until cool.
3. Sweeten if desired; serve over ice.

Cucumber–Lime Sparkling Water

Prep	Cook	Servings
5 min	0 min	4

Nutrition (per serving): 15 cal · 0 g protein · 0 g fiber · 0 mg sodium

Ingredients

- ½ cucumber, thinly sliced
- ½ lime, sliced
- 2 cups sparkling water
- A few fresh mint leaves (optional)

Flavor Twist: Infuse with mint or ginger for a zesty, cooling refreshment.

Instructions

1. Add cucumber, lime, and mint to a pitcher or glass.
2. Pour in sparkling water and stir gently to combine flavors.
3. Chill for 5 minutes, then serve cold for a crisp, refreshing drink.

Apple–Cinnamon Herbal Infusion

Prep	Cook	Servings
5 min	10 min	4

Nutrition (per serving): 30 cal · 0 g protein · 1 g fiber · 0 mg sodium

Ingredients

- 1 small apple, thinly sliced
- 1 cinnamon stick
- 2 cups hot water
- 1 teaspoon honey (optional)

Flavor Twist: Include orange peel or cloves for a cozy, spiced aroma.

Instructions

1. Place apple slices and cinnamon stick in a mug or teapot.
2. Pour hot water over and steep for 5–7 minutes.
3. Remove cinnamon, sweeten with honey and enjoy warm.

Ginger–Lemon Morning Tonic

Strawberry–Basil Infused Water

Prep	Cook	Servings
3 min	7 min	2

Nutrition (per serving): 20 cal · 0 g protein · 0 g fiber · 0 mg sodium

Prep	Cook	Servings
5 min	0 min	4

Nutrition (per serving): 25 cal · 0 g protein · 1 g fiber · 0 mg sodium

Ingredients

- 1 teaspoon freshly grated ginger
- 1 tablespoon lemon juice
- 2 cups warm water
- 1 teaspoon honey (optional)

Flavor Twist: Add mint or cayenne for a bright, energizing morning boost.

Ingredients

- 4 fresh strawberries, sliced
- 3 fresh basil leaves
- 2 cups cold water
- Ice cubes (optional)

Flavor Twist: Add a squeeze of lemon or a few cucumber slices for extra freshness.

Instructions

1. Add grated ginger and lemon juice to a mug.
2. Pour in warm water and then stir well.
3. Add honey if desired, then sip slowly to start your day bright.

Instructions

1. Add strawberries and basil leaves to a pitcher or glass.
2. Pour in cold water and stir gently to release flavor.
3. Let sit 10 minutes or chill with ice before enjoying.

Blueberry–Lavender Calm Tea

Prep	Cook	Servings
5 min	5 min	4

Nutrition (per serving): 30 cal · 0 g protein · 1 g fiber · 0 mg sodium

Ingredients

- 🧑‍🍳 ½ cup blueberries, halved
- 🧑‍🍳 ½ tsp dried lavender
- 🧑‍🍳 4 cups water

Flavor Twist: Stir in a touch of honey or add a slice of pear for gentle sweetness.

Instructions

1. Steep lavender in hot water 5 min.
2. Add blueberries; chill or serve warm.
3. Enjoy soothing flavor

Iced Green Tea with Citrus & Mint

Prep	Cook	Servings
5 min	3 min	4

Nutrition (per serving): 30 cal · 0 g protein · 1 g fiber · 0 mg sodium

Ingredients

- 🧑‍🍳 2 green tea bags
- 🧑‍🍳 ½ orange, sliced
- 🧑‍🍳 6 mint leaves

Flavor Twist: Mix in orange slices or a splash of sparkling water for a lively lift.

Instructions

1. Steep tea bags in 4 cups of hot water for 3 min.
2. Add orange and mint.
3. Chill for 15 minutes and then serve cold.

Peach–Rosemary Spritzer

Spiced Apple–Ginger Warmer

Prep	Cook	Servings
5 min	0 min	4

Nutrition (per serving): 35 cal · 0 g protein · 1 g fiber · 0 mg sodium

Prep	Cook	Servings
5 min	10 min	3

Nutrition (per serving): 60 cal · 0 g protein · 1 g fiber · 5 mg sodium

Ingredients

Ingredients

- 1 ripe peach, sliced
- 1 sprig rosemary
- 4 cups sparkling water
- Raspberries (optional)

Flavor Twist: Add a few raspberries or a hint of lemon juice for bright balance.

- 2 cups apple cider (low-sugar if possible)
- 1-inch ginger, sliced
- 1 cinnamon stick with 2 cloves

Flavor Twist: Include a pinch of nutmeg or orange zest for cozy seasonal depth.

Instructions

Instructions

1. Add sliced peaches and fresh rosemary sprigs to a large pitcher.
2. Pour in chilled sparkling water and stir lightly.
3. Let it set for 15 minutes and then serve cold as a fizzy refreshment.

1. Combine apple cider, sliced ginger, and spices in a small pot.
2. Bring to a gentle simmer and cook for about 10 minutes to infuse flavor.
3. Strain into mugs and serve hot for a cozy, aromatic drink.

Coconut–Pineapple Refresher

Chamomile–Vanilla Evening Tea

Prep	Cook	Servings
5 min	0 min	2

Nutrition (per serving): 90 cal · 1 g protein · 2 g fiber · 15 mg sodium

Prep	Cook	Servings
3 min	5 min	2

Nutrition (per serving): 20 cal · 0 g protein · 0 g fiber · 0 mg sodium

Ingredients

- 1 cup coconut water
- 1 cup pineapple juice
- 1 tbsp shredded coconut (optional)

Flavor Twist: Blend with a squeeze of lime or a few mint leaves for tropical zest.

Ingredients

- 2 chamomile tea bags
- ½ tsp vanilla extract
- 1 tsp honey (optional)
- 2 cups hot water

Flavor Twist: Add a dash of cinnamon or a spoon of warm milk for soothing comfort.

Instructions

1. Stir coconut water and pineapple juice.
2. Sprinkle with coconut if using.
3. Serve cool or over ice.

Instructions

1. Steep chamomile tea bags in hot water 5 min.
2. Stir in vanilla and honey if desired.
3. Serve warm; best enjoyed before bedtime.

Snacks and Small Bites

Red Pepper & Walnut Spread

Prep	Cook	Servings
8 min	10 min	1

Nutrition (per serving): 120 cal · 3 g protein · 2 g fiber · 140 mg sodium

Ingredients

- 2 red bell peppers, roasted
- ¼ cup walnuts
- 1 tbsp olive oil
- ½ tsp paprika

Flavor Twist: Add a squeeze of lemon or a pinch of smoked paprika

Instructions

1. Roast peppers until skins blister; peel.
2. Blend with walnuts, oil, and paprika.
3. Serve with whole-grain crackers.

Garlic Spread and Crackers

Prep	Cook	Servings
5 min	0 min	1

Nutrition (per serving): 100 cal · 5 g protein · 4 g fiber · 120 mg sodium

Ingredients

- 1 cup canned white beans
- 1 garlic clove, minced
- 1 tbsp olive oil
- Juice of ½ lemon

Flavor Twist: Mix in roasted red pepper or a dash of cumin

Instructions

1. Blend beans, garlic, oil, and lemon juice.
2. Spread on whole-grain crackers and serve cool for a light, satisfying snack.

Cottage Cheese & Peach Bowl

Roasted Edamame with Smoked Paprika

Prep	Cook	Servings
8 min	10 min	1

Nutrition (per serving): 120 cal · 3 g protein · 2 g fiber · 140 mg sodium

Prep	Cook	Servings
5 min	0 min	1

Nutrition (per serving): 100 cal · 5 g protein · 4 g fiber · 120 mg sodium

Ingredients

- 1 cup low-fat cottage cheese
- 1 peach, sliced
- 1 tbsp chopped almonds
- Cinnamon (optional)

Flavor Twist: Sprinkle cinnamon or crushed almonds for crunch.

Ingredients

- 2 cups frozen shelled edamame, thawed
- 1 tbsp olive oil
- ½ tsp smoked paprika

Flavor Twist: Add a dash of garlic powder or chili flakes for extra zest.

Instructions

1. Divide cottage cheese into bowls.
2. Top with peach slices and almonds
3. Drizzle lightly with honey

Instructions

1. Toss edamame with oil and paprika.
2. Spread on baking sheet and roast at 400°F for 15 min until crisp.

Crispy Chickpea Bites with Herbs

Prep	Cook	Servings
5 min	20 min	

Nutrition (per serving): 140 cal · 6 g protein · 5 g fiber · 160 mg sodium

Ingredients

- 1 can chickpeas, rinsed and dried
- 1 tbsp olive oil
- ½ tsp dried thyme
- ½ tsp dried oregano
- Lemon juice (optional)

Flavor Twist: Toss with lemon juice and parsley for a fresh Mediterranean touch.

Instructions

1. Toss chickpeas with oil and herbs.
2. Roast at 400°F for 20 min, shaking pan halfway.
3. Serve warm and crunchy as an evening snack.

Baked Sweet Potato Fries

Prep	Cook	Servings
8 min	18 min	2

Nutrition (per serving): 210 cal · 6 g protein · 5 g fiber · 180 mg sodium

Ingredients

- 1 large potato, cut into fries
- 1 tbsp olive oil
- ½ tsp paprika
- ½ cup Greek yogurt
- 1 tsp fresh dill, chopped

Flavor Twist: Sprinkle with cinnamon or cayenne for a sweet–spicy balance.

Instructions

1. Toss fries with oil and paprika.
2. Bake at 425°F for 18 min until golden.
3. Mix yogurt with dill and serve as a dill.

Roasted Carrot Sticks

Baked Zucchini Chips

Prep	Cook	Servings
7 min	18 min	2

Nutrition (per serving): 160 cal · 6 g protein · 4 g fiber · 150 mg sodium

Prep	Cook	Servings
7 min	15 min	2

Nutrition (per serving): 140 cal · 8 g protein · 3 g fiber · 190 mg sodium

Ingredients

Ingredients

- ♟ 2 large carrots, cut into sticks
- ♟ 1 tbsp olive oil
- ♟ ½ tsp thyme
- ♟ ½ cup Greek yogurt
- ♟ 1 tsp lemon juice

Flavor Twist: Drizzle with honey and thyme for a gently caramelized finish.

- ♟ 2 small zucchinis, thinly sliced into even rounds
- ♟ 2 tbsp grated Parmesan
- ♟ 1 tbsp olive oil
- ♟ Garlic powder (optional)

Flavor Twist: Dust with garlic powder for a savory crunch.

Instructions

Instructions

1. Preheat oven to 400°F (200°C).
2. Toss carrots with oil, salt, pepper, and thyme.
3. Roast 20–25 minutes until tender and golden.

1. Toss zucchini with oil and Parmesan.
2. Spread slices on baking sheet.
3. Bake at 425°F for 15 min until crisp.

Hummus–Cucumber Roll-Ups

Prep	Cook	Servings
5 min	0 min	8

Nutrition (per serving): 110 cal · 5 g protein · 3 g fiber · 140 mg sodium

Ingredients

- ♟ 8 cucumber strips (peeled lengthwise)
- ♟ 4 tbsp hummus
- ♟ 2 tbsp shredded carrots

Flavor Twist: Add shredded carrots or sprinkle dill for extra texture and flavor.

Instructions

1. Spread hummus on tortillas.
2. Add cucumber slices.
3. Roll tightly, slice, and chill before serving.

Mini Pita Pizzas with Spinach & Tomato

Prep	Cook	Servings
5 min	10 min	4

Nutrition (per serving): 220 cal · 11 g protein · 4 g fiber · 260 mg sodium

Ingredients

- ♟ 2 whole-grain pitas, halved
- ♟ ½ cup spinach, chopped
- ♟ ½ cup cherry tomatoes, halved
- ♟ ¼ cup mozzarella, shredded

Flavor Twist: Add crumbled feta or a drizzle of pesto for rich Mediterranean flair.

Instructions

1. Top pita halves with spinach, tomatoes, and cheese.
2. Bake at 400°F for 8–10 min until cheese melts and serve.

Peach & Almond Energy Bites

Stuffed Cherry Tomatoes

Prep	Cook	Servings
8 min	0 min	12

Nutrition (per serving): 150 cal · 5 g protein · 3 g fiber · 90 mg sodium

Prep	Cook	Servings
7 min	0 min	12

Nutrition (per serving): 90 cal · 6 g protein · 2 g fiber · 120 mg sodium

Ingredients

Ingredients

- ½ cup dried peaches, chopped
- ½ cup rolled oats
- ¼ cup almond butter
- 2 tbsp chopped almonds
- 1 tsp honey

Flavor Twist: Mix in shredded coconut or a few dried cranberries for natural sweetness.

- 12 cherry tomatoes
- ½ cup cottage cheese
- 1 tsp fresh parsley, chopped
- 1 tsp chives, chopped
- Basil (optional)

Flavor Twist: Add chopped basil or a sprinkle of feta for a bright, tangy twist.

Instructions

Instructions

1. Blend peaches, oats, almond butter, almonds, and honey.
2. Roll into 12 small balls.
3. Chill 20 min; serve cool.

1. Hollow out cherry tomatoes.
2. Mix cottage cheese with parsley and chives.
3. Spoon into tomatoes; serve fresh.

Delightful & DASH Desserts

Citrus Yogurt Parfait

Prep	Cook	Servings
5 min	0 min	1

Nutrition (per serving): 160 cal · 9 g protein · 2 g fiber · 90 mg sodium

Ingredients

- ¾ cup low-fat Greek yogurt
- ½ orange, segmented
- 1 tbsp oats
- 1 tsp honey

Flavor Twist: Add pistachios and orange zest for a twist.

Instructions

1. Spoon creamy yogurt into a glass or bowl, spreading it evenly.
2. Add fresh orange segments on top, then sprinkle with oats
3. Drizzle lightly with honey and serve fresh for a bright, energizing treat.

Berry–Nut Oat Bars

Prep	Cook	Servings
7 min	15 min	6

Nutrition (per serving): 190 cal · 6 g protein · 4 g fiber · 120 mg sodium

Ingredients

- 1 cup rolled oats
- ½ cup mixed berries
- ¼ cup almonds, chopped
- 2 tbsp honey

Flavor Twist: Swirl in almond butter and drizzle dark chocolate.

Instructions

1. Preheat oven to 350°F (175°C).
2. Mix oats, berries, almonds, honey.
3. Press in lined pan, bake 15 min.
4. Cool, slice into bars.

Choco Almond Clusters

Prep	Cook	Servings
5 min	5 min	8

Nutrition (per serving): 150 cal · 6 g protein · 3 g fiber · 80 mg sodium

Ingredients

- ½ cup dark chocolate chips
- ½ cup almonds, unsalted
- 1 tsp honey (optional)
- Pinch sea salt (optional)

Flavor Twist: Mix in dried cherries for a sweet, tangy flavor boost.

Instructions

1. Melt chocolate.
2. Mix in almonds and honey (optional).
3. Drop spoonful on parchment.
4. Sprinkle salt if desired, chill 20 min until firm.

Blueberry–Lemon Yogurt Whip

Prep	Cook	Servings
6 min	0 min	2

Nutrition (per serving): 140 cal · 8 g protein · 2 g fiber · 85 mg sodium

Ingredients

- 1 cup low-fat Greek yogurt
- ½ cup blueberries
- 1 tsp honey
- ½ tsp lemon zest

Flavor Twist: Fold in crushed graham crackers for a twist.

Instructions

1. Stir yogurt, honey, and lemon zest until smooth.
2. Fold in blueberries.
3. Chill 10 min before serving.

Spiced Compote with Walnuts

Baked Apple with Cinnamon

Prep	Cook	Servings
7 min	8 min	2

Nutrition (per serving): 160 cal · 4 g protein · 3 g fiber · 80 mg sodium

Prep	Cook	Servings
5 min	15 min	2

Nutrition (per serving): 170 cal · 3 g protein · 4 g fiber · 95 mg sodium

Ingredients

Ingredients

- 2 ripe pears, diced
- 1 tsp honey
- ¼ tsp cinnamon
- 2 tbsp walnuts, chopped

Flavor Twist: Add a splash of vanilla and orange zest for warmth.

- 1 apple, halved and cored
- 2 tbsp rolled oats
- 1 tsp honey
- ¼ tsp cinnamon

Flavor Twist: Top with crushed pecans and drizzle maple syrup.

Instructions

Instructions

1. Cook pears in a small pan 6–8 min until soft.
2. Stir in honey and cinnamon.
3. Top with walnuts.
4. Serve warm or chilled.

1. Preheat oven to 375°F (190°C).
2. Fill apple halves with oats, honey, and cinnamon.
3. Bake 15 min until tender.

Raspberry–Pudding

Prep	Cook	Servings
5 min	0 min	2

Nutrition (per serving): 150 cal · 6 g protein · 6 g fiber · 70 mg sodium

Ingredients

- 2 tbsp chia seeds
- 1 cup low-fat milk
- ½ tsp vanilla extract
- ½ cup raspberries

Flavor Twist: Blend in shredded coconut for a tropical twist.

Instructions

1. Stir chia seeds, milk, and vanilla in a jar until evenly combined.

2. Refrigerate 2 hours until thick and creamy, stirring once midway.

3. Top with fresh raspberries and serve chilled for a light, refreshing treat.

Honey Bark with Nuts

Prep	Cook	Servings
6 min	0 min	8

Nutrition (per serving): 160 cal · 8 g protein · 2 g fiber · 75 mg sodium

Ingredients

- 1 cup low-fat Greek yogurt
- 1 tbsp honey
- 2 tbsp mixed nuts, chopped
- ¼ cup berries

Flavor Twist: Sprinkle with sea salt and orange zest.

Instructions

1. Spread yogurt onto a parchment-lined tray.

2. Drizzle honey and sprinkle nuts and berries.

3. Freeze 2 hrs until firm.

4. Break into pieces and serve cold.

Baked Apricot Halves

Prep	Cook	Servings
5 min	12 min	2

Nutrition (per serving): 150 cal · 4 g protein · 3 g fiber · 65 mg sodium

Ingredients

- 2 fresh apricots, halved
- 2 tsp honey
- 2 tbsp almonds, chopped
- ¼ tsp cinnamon

Flavor Twist: Drizzle with honey and top with crushed pistachios.

Instructions

1. Preheat oven to 375°F (190°C).
2. Place apricots cut-side up in a dish.
3. Drizzle honey, sprinkle cinnamon and almonds.
4. Bake 12 min until tender.

Cocoa–Banana Mousse

Prep	Cook	Servings
5 min	0 min	2

Nutrition (per serving): 170 cal · 5 g protein · 5 g fiber · 85 mg sodium

Ingredients

- 1 banana, mashed
- 1 cup low-fat milk
- 2 tbsp chia seeds
- 1 tbsp cocoa powder

Flavor Twist: Add a pinch of cinnamon and espresso.

Instructions

1. Blend banana, milk, and cocoa until smooth.
2. Stir in chia seeds.
3. Refrigerate 1 hr. until mousse-like. Serve chilled.

Honey Yoghurt Cups

Prep	Cook	Servings
6 min	0 min	6

Nutrition (per serving): 140 cal · 7 g protein · 2 g fiber · 70 mg sodium

Ingredients

- 🧑‍🍳 1 cup low-fat Greek yogurt
- 🧑‍🍳 2 tsp honey
- 🧑‍🍳 ½ tsp vanilla extract
- 🧑‍🍳 ¼ cup diced fruit

Flavor Twist: Layer with crushed almonds and figs for a twist.

Instructions

1. Spoon yogurt into cups.
2. Drizzle with honey.
3. Top with sliced fruit and crushed nuts.
4. Chill briefly before serving cool and creamy.

Strawberry Almond Cups

Prep	Cook	Servings
10 min	20 min	2

Nutrition (per serving): 150 cal · 6 g protein · 3 g fiber · 80 mg sodium

Ingredients

- 🧑‍🍳 1 cup low-fat Greek yogurt
- 🧑‍🍳 ½ cup strawberries, chopped
- 🧑‍🍳 2 tbsp almonds, chopped
- 🧑‍🍳 2 tsp honey

Flavor Twist: Drizzle with dark chocolate and add mint.

Instructions

1. Layer yogurt in cups.
2. Add sliced strawberries and a drizzle of honey.
3. Sprinkle chopped almonds on top.
4. Serve chilled and fresh.

DASH Tools for Everyday Success

Healthy eating is easier when the right tools are at your fingertips. This final section brings together simple guides and checklists to keep the DASH lifestyle practical day after day. These tools are designed to save time, reduce stress, and make every meal more enjoyable.

Your Gentle 4-Week Meal Path

Week 1

Breakfast	Lunch	Dinner
Citrus Yogurt Parfait	Greek Chickpea Salad	Lemon–Garlic Baked Cod with Spinach
Cornmeal Mini Pancakes	Warm Barley & Mushroom Salad	Herb–Crusted Tilapia with Dijon
Bell Pepper Egg Skillet	Refreshing Watermelon–Cucumber Salad	One-Pan Chicken with Rosemary & Apples
Cheddar–Broccoli Egg Cups	Tuna & White Bean Salad	Mushroom–Asparagus Brown Rice Skillet
Vanilla Chia Cups	Cabbage–Carrot Slaw	Garlic–Herb Trout with Lemon
Zucchini–Potato Hash	Roasted Beet & Walnut Salad	Simple Lentil–Sweet Potato Bowl
Golden Turmeric Latte + Oat Bar	Summer Strawberry & Spinach Salad	Shrimp Stir-Fry with Snap Peas & Carrots

Week 2

Breakfast	Lunch	Dinner
Berry–Nut Yogurt Crunch Bowl	Roasted Zucchini & Tomato Salad	Turkey–Tomato Skillet
Cinnamon Rice Bowl	Apple–Walnut Kale Slaw	Grilled Mackerel with Swiss Chard
Pear–Ginger Smoothie	Creamy Tomato–Basil Soup	Cauliflower–Garlic Mash with Pasta
Almond–Date Energy Bites	Quinoa–Kale Bowl	Easy Turkey Meatballs with Tomato–Basil Sauce
Strawberry–Almond Frozen Cups	Summer Strawberry & Spinach Salad	Chicken & Tomato Bake with Olives
Cheddar–Broccoli Egg Cups	Greek Chickpea Salad	Grilled Eggplant with Mozzarella
Vanilla Chia Cups	Refreshing Watermelon–Cucumber Salad	Pumpkin–Red Lentil Stew

Week 3

Breakfast	Lunch	Dinner
Cottage Cheese & Pear Bowl	Roasted Beet & Walnut Salad	Garlic–Herb Trout with Lemon

Cornmeal Mini Pancakes	Cabbage–Carrot Slaw	Lemon–Garlic Baked Cod with Spinach
Berry–Nut Yogurt Crunch Bowl	Summer Strawberry & Spinach Salad	Simple Lentil–Sweet Potato Bowl
Zucchini–Potato Hash	Greek Chickpea Salad	Shrimp Stir-Fry with Snap Peas & Carrots
Vanilla Chia Cups	Warm Barley & Mushroom Salad	Mushroom–Asparagus Brown Rice Skillet
Citrus Yogurt Parfait	Apple–Walnut Kale Slaw	Herb–Crusted Tilapia with Dijon
Pear–Ginger Smoothie	Creamy Tomato–Basil Soup	One-Pan Chicken with Rosemary & Apples

Week 4

Breakfast	Lunch	Dinner
Golden Turmeric Latte + Oat Bar	Refreshing Watermelon–Cucumber Salad	Grilled Eggplant with Mozzarella
Cheddar–Broccoli Egg Cups	Roasted Zucchini & Tomato Salad	Turkey–Tomato Skillet
Almond–Date Energy Bites	Quinoa–Kale Bowl	Chicken & Tomato Bake with Olives
Cinnamon Rice Bowl	Summer Strawberry & Spinach Salad	Garlic–Herb Trout with Lemon

Vanilla Chia Cups	Roasted Beet & Walnut Salad	Cauliflower–Garlic Mash with Pasta
Berry–Nut Yogurt Crunch Bowl	Tuna & White Bean Salad	Pumpkin–Red Lentil Stew
Pear–Ginger Smoothie	Apple–Walnut Kale Slaw	Grilled Mackerel with Swiss Chard

Sodium & Blood Pressure Tracker

How to Use: Track meals, note sodium when possible, and record blood pressure once or twice daily. Over time, you'll spot progress and patterns to discuss with your doctor.

Date	Meals and Snacks	Estimated sodium	Estimated Blood Pressure

Senior Swaps: Gentle Adjustments for Everyday Cooking

Cooking should be enjoyable, not tiring. These simple swaps make DASH meals easier to chew, lighter on spice, and quicker to prepare—without losing flavor or nutrition.

Easy Chewing

- Swap **raw carrots or apples** → for **steamed carrots or soft pears/peaches**.
- Swap **crusty bread** → for **soft whole-grain tortillas or oat bread**.
- Swap **tough greens (kale, collards)** → for **spinach or cooked zucchini**.

Milder Spices

- Swap **hot chili flakes or cayenne** → for **mild paprika or cinnamon**.
- Swap **raw onion or garlic** → for **roasted onion or garlic powder** (gentler on digestion).
- Swap **vinegar-heavy dressings** → for **lemon juice or yogurt-based dressings**.

Low-Effort Prep

- Swap **chopping fresh herbs** → for **dried herbs or frozen herb cubes**.
- Swap **peeling and dicing potatoes** → for **pre-cut frozen sweet potato cubes**.
- Swap **washing and trimming greens** → for **bagged spinach or salad mixes**.

Pantry Essentials at a Glance

Grains: Brown rice, oats, whole-grain pasta, whole-wheat bread.

Proteins: Canned tuna or salmon, beans, lentils, eggs.

Produce: Low-sodium canned tomatoes, frozen spinach, fresh apples, pears, bananas.

Flavor Builders: Olive oil, lemon juice, garlic, onion, black pepper, herbs (basil, dill, parsley).

Snacks: Unsalted nuts, plain yogurt, whole-grain crackers.

CONCLUSION

Every meal is more than food on a plate. It is a step toward better days ahead. By choosing simple, nourishing dishes, you are giving your body steady strength and your mind greater peace. The DASH way of eating is not about restriction but about possibility.

Each recipe in this book is meant to remind you that healthy eating does not have to be complicated. With a few fresh ingredients and a little care, you can prepare meals that are gentle on the body yet full of flavor. These meals support your health today and protect your well-being for the future.

Whether you are cooking for yourself, sharing with loved ones, or trying a new recipe for the first time, each bite is a chance to feel lighter, stronger, and more alive. Small daily choices can open the door to years filled with energy, independence, and joy.

The journey does not end here. This is the beginning of new opportunities to explore flavors, to enjoy health, and to live each day with vitality and confidence. It is never too late to care for yourself, to build new habits, and to discover foods that make you feel good inside and out.

Your future is not behind you. It is waiting at the table, in every fresh meal, and in every new moment you choose to embrace. The best chapters of life can still unfold, one wholesome plate at a time.

So, take these recipes with you as companions, not just instructions. Let them guide you, comfort you, and remind you that every day holds the promise of nourishment, renewal, and joy. Here's to many more meals, memories, and moments ahead.

Printed in Dunstable, United Kingdom

74263104R00051